Reclaiming Me
LOST INNOCENCE

A true story about grooming
and sexual abuse, and the
strength it took to become
the light in the storm.

ATHENA TEMPEST ROSE

Reclaiming Me: Lost Innocence

Copyright © 2022 Athena Tempest Rose.
Produced and printed by Stillwater River Publications. All rights reserved. Written and produced in the United States of America. This book may not be reproduced or sold in any form without the expressed, written permission of the author(s) and publisher.

Visit our website at **www.StillwaterPress.com** for more information.

First Stillwater River Publications Edition.

ISBN: 978-1-958217-33-7 *(paperback)*
ISBN: 978-1-958217-75-7 *(hardback)*

Library of Congress Control Number: 2022912631

1 2 3 4 5 6 7 8 9 10
Written by Athena Tempest Rose.
Cover and interior design by Elisha Gillette.
Published by Stillwater River Publications, Pawtucket, RI, USA.

Names: Rose, Athena Tempest, author.
Title: Reclaiming me : lost innocence / Athena Tempest Rose.
Description: First Stillwater River Publications edition. | Pawtucket, RI, USA : Stillwater River Publications, [2022]
Identifiers: ISBN: 978-1-958217-33-7 | LCCN: 2022912631
Subjects: LCSH: Rose, Athena Tempest. | Sexual abuse victims--Biography. | Sexual abuse victims--Psychology. | Manipulative behavior. | Post-traumatic stress disorder. | Courage. | LCGFT: Autobiographies.
Classification: LCC: HV6625 .R67 2022 | DDC: 362.883--dc23

The views and opinions expressed in this book are solely those of the author(s) and do not necessarily reflect the views and opinions of the publisher.

Reclaiming Me
Lost Innocence

Introduction

Who am I?

After years of blogging, trying to figure out what exactly I'm hoping to help others understand and learn, I have realized it was me who also needed to learn. What follows is my story, which remains unfinished. Through my writings and therapy I realized how much of my younger years were spent in what I will call a survival state. This state protected me from the worst parts of my life, but also prevented me from developing a healthy image of myself and the world around me.

If this is the first time you've heard of me I'm not surprised, but also thank you for reading. Why should you spend the money or time to read what I have to say? When I first started my website, I would have said, "I don't know." At that time, I also didn't realize that a better part of my preteen through young adult life was controlled by a man that was ten years my senior. I was groomed, but had no clue until after my forty-second birthday.

What I did know is that I'd spent my life trying to fit into a world I was watching from the outside, but knowing I would never quite fit in. *Believe* me. I could donate to a bake sale, volunteer at every church or school event, look like a happy wife and mother, and support my friends. I could smile and nod, but my head was always in the clouds. Well, until I chose to push through the storm and take my happiness into my own hands.

I have lived my life on my own timetable. The day I was born my mother was playing softball. Why would she do otherwise? I wasn't supposed to be coming till November. Instead, it was the beginning of September when her water broke. At the hospital they placed a monitor on me in utero while pushing steroids to prepare my lungs to work. My mom was left in a wheelchair in the hallway. When my father arrived, he questioned whether I was even his. In my early thirties, I did DNA testing and there is no question I am biologically his.

After my father arrived, my mother stated I was coming now. The doctors and nurses were nowhere to be found so she placed her hands under my head and delivered me in the wheelchair. Because I weighed over five pounds, they were not worried about me coming early. However, it was a problem. My lungs were not fully developed, so I was given my last rites at a couple months old. I definitely wasn't ready to go. I showed the fighting spirit which I would need for the rest of my life. Through this book, I hope to take you on a journey of my life, the things that happened to me, and how I persevered despite those things. What matters most is not what happens to us but how we react and how we choose to move forward.

If you don't know what I've been through, most would say I chose the wrong men, women, or people; I have bad luck; or Buddha, God, or whoever you believe in is trying to test me. That's what I thought as well when I started writing. I believed everything was my fault. I couldn't figure out how to be a good partner or be enough for someone. The one thing I did know was no matter what, how I chose to move forward in life was my choice. Choosing my path has caused my strength to waver time and time again, because I couldn't always see my worth through the tempest, but it is, and always has been, the light in the storm. No matter what gets thrown at me I will keep moving forward with love and light. Yes, I do fall and cry and not want to get up sometimes, but I will get up and continue to shine a light in the darkness.

Why would I even bother to write about my life? And why now? Because I'm just starting to put the pieces together. My abuse was so ingrained in me that I didn't see it for what it was, but it affected everything in my life. I know I'm not alone, which is why my voice is no longer staying quiet! **I am speaking up so that way those still silenced can know that they deserve love and respect for who they are.** You may feel broken right now, but you are strong and amazing. Nothing that happened is your fault!

For me I started healing by going back to journaling. As I did I realized how much of my life was locked away due to dissociation. I had spent years trying to block out everything that had happened. Which in my early thirties felt like I was finally okay and safe. That was until the man I loved changed into someone else. At thirty-eight I had to start all over again and this time with even more fear.

December 2018

How does one start feeling when their whole life was spent learning how to avoid feelings? Block out fear and pain.

My life has been a shit show the past few weeks, months, and years. Because of mental illness and rape, I have lost my husband who supposedly loved me. Two years ago, I thought we would be together forever and that nothing could stop that. Until I had surgery in March 2017. I woke up to doctors telling me I might die and that they didn't know what was going on. I turned to faith and exercise... he got scared and decided that it was okay to be verbally and sexually abusive. Because, after all, I was his property. This wasn't the first time I had been abused in my life and wasn't even the last. Nevertheless, despite being told what was happening, I still couldn't see it for myself. His sister, who had become my sister over the years, told me multiple times to get him out of the house. She probably saved me and my kids' lives. I've struggled every day since, wondering if I deserved to be loved and thinking I caused all of the abuse. There must be something wrong with me. I always end up in abusive relationships. It's like I don't know how to choose the nice guy. But Marc was "the nice guy." How did he become a monster?

More importantly, how do I know what to do next? If I explore my past will I be able to handle it? How do I help myself? How does that affect my children? Will writing help or will it make me even more scared to leave my house?

I started exploring those questions and multitudes more when I opened up Pandora's box, which for me was writing and taking ownership of my thoughts and the direction of my life.

Where Do I Start?

I feel that if I start deep in the recesses of my childhood no one will really want to read. Too much deep shit and not a hell of a lot of fun. So how about we start with where I started, the blog, and mix in the making of Athena as we go? Then I'll bring you back to where it all began.

The year was 2017, and the name Athena came from *Game of War*, a group strategy game that allowed me to escape my life: four kids, a hysterectomy, complications from surgery, gastroparesis, being financially dependent on my dad, and a husband that couldn't handle my changing health. Even as I type this, I feel that grip of fear and of not knowing what to do. I saw my life spiraling out of control, so I took control in the only way I could: a game with all interactions taking place in chat rooms or just on-screen game chat.

When I started playing *Game of War*, the alliance exclusively talked in game. That turned into Line chat rooms, a social media application where things ran like a middle school cafeteria—you could be popular one day and booted the next. People in these rooms ranged from hardcore gamers who had no other social lives, to those just having fun, and all the way to those who were escaping their home lives. I was in the latter when I started getting invited to nongaming rooms it seemed like a perfect escape, well at the time.

Except...consent?

Consent is a moving target in the world of social media. We

talk about consent in so many different ways. First, minors can't give consent for nudes; if you send or receive pictures or videos of minors being sexualized you can go to jail no matter what your age! Adults sending me a penis picture or requiring me to show photographic "proof" of what I'm doing is actually quite terrifying for most people. This also is likely nonconsensual and starts making things gray. Can I say no to a proof rule? Or lock down my personal messages to prevent anyone from sending me pictures I don't want?

Social media chat rooms were one of my first places to watch and ask questions when I started learning about the Lifestyle. More and more of these rooms are requiring either personal verification of age or some form of live picture with a license, or just the date and verbal confirmation of age. This is meant to try to exclude minors but we all know if a minor wants in, they are more tech savvy than most of the adults. As an adult, if you run any chat rooms you need to do your best to vet people and keep minors out of adult-themed chat rooms; you could even be held liable if you just "didn't know they were under eighteen."

Social media becomes an escape for many, but knowing how to navigate it can get messy. Lifestyle social media tends to be even more messy. These chat rooms also throw more information at you than anyone should. No topic, picture, or video is off-limits. Group chats with videos…yes, imagine truth or dare on steroids. Be careful what you say. If you accidentally mention that you were in the bath when you were reading, someone may call "proof." If proof is called then you are strongly encouraged to show "proof" that you are/were indeed in the bath or risk being kicked out of the room. Most get really good at taking pictures of their feet or the edge of the tub, but others take a full body shot.

Does that sound truly consensual? There is no asking, but you entered the room. Most rooms have some type of rules set. If you don't like it, you could leave, but if you have friends in those rooms, how does that work?

I say I lost myself in it, but unless you've ever been involved in a game like this where groups of people work together to defeat their opponents, you probably don't realize just how much those people in your "alliance" become part of your family. I became the natural leader and with that, the Goddess of War was born.

Before I even accepted this name, my game family had started calling me Athena. When I say "family," we talked via chat groups and phone calls every day and when someone got sick or was struggling we all tried to help each other. Boxes of children's clothes sent to Florida, a GoFundMe set up for a member's hospital bills, and locals helping clear property after hurricanes. When one of our members passed away, we all pitched in to send a donation to a veteran's group in her name. Now, five years later I still have contact with a handful of the people I "met" through this escape. I still consider them family and friends.

One member of my Line family is Wayward. She is an amazing woman who I've known for over five years through Line, helped me start my website, pushed her way into my heart like no other woman ever has. What does that mean? Wayward and I both have needs that have not been met in other relationships. However, we have never met in person. How can we have a relationship on opposite sides of the country? Also, since we are polyamorous, what are the rules? The following is just a little glimpse of what our contract and relationship looked like in 2019. We did not want to look back and have what-ifs over our heads.

Wayward and I love with our hearts open. Wayward presents a tough exterior trying to show the world that she doesn't get pushed around by others, but that is only what she shows to the world. If she loves you, she would do anything you ask of her even if it means sacrificing part of herself. I see that, and for some reason, she trusts me with her heart. So much so that I know certain decisions I could force on her but then I would know someday, maybe not today but one day in the future, she may grow to despise me and think "What if..?" One of the other ways she shows her love is by being fiercely protective of me and I don't mean telling me I can't do things. She wants me to go out and have fun and explore the possibility of being with others. Her protection is coming from an amazing place where if a guy oversteps his boundaries towards me, even if it's accidental, she puts him in his place. A friend of hers has been flirting with me—they have slept together—and he sent me a picture of his penis. I sent it to her because we told each other everything and his timing had sucked. I had just said I was playing with kids and bam! it was there. She wrote him a text that said if you do that shit again I will come and punch you. She didn't say what I was so used to hearing: "You must have said something to deserve it." Instead she shut him down saying, "It was inappropriate." That alone made me feel amazing.

I, on the other hand, allow others into my life emotionally way too easily. I give myself to those who ask for help or tell me I'm special. I want to be loved in the same way I love others. I believe that people are inherently good, so I see the good in them until someone else points out the flaws, or occasionally I'll notice them myself. However, I am more prone to miss red flags until they're pointed out to me.

There was one time when a ghost from my and Wayward's past showed up and shook us both. Then a male I thought liked me for me ripped me apart. These two events shook me and had me confused, which often leads to me disassociating to protect myself. I then went on Fetlife and for the first time responded to someone's request to talk. He told me he wasn't the kind to rush things. However, within a few hours he wanted my phone number, FB account, and friends' names, who I was hanging out with. There should have been flags in my head, but no; at the time I thought it was because I was emotionally fried and he had "good reasons" for wanting them: to get to know me.

Wayward was there and was like, "Please don't, Hun. It's too good to be true and he's sending red flags." I didn't see it but promised her I would push back a little. I did and he flipped, but still I thought it was my fear because of my history. Then morning came and he was all over me, even while I was still happily sleeping on the other side of the phone from Wayward. He wanted me to send nudes for my "Daddy." The good thing is even I know that's a red flag—so I said no. He immediately said that wasn't allowed and blamed me for being too damaged to have a relationship. Even though I know in my head that he had the problem because that's not how submission works, I still in my heart feel I am too broken to be cared for.

Wayward and I each have our rough patches, sometimes for the same reasons and sometimes for different reasons, but I know she will sit on a call with me just to listen to me cry or sleep when I can't fall asleep alone. I can help her come back after a panic attack or stop it by just listening and talking. We were each other's support while the world around us pushed us around. It doesn't matter what happens; I know that as long as we continue to keep our relationship full of honesty, trust, respect, and communication we will be okay.

We both knew that creating a way to help people heal from grooming and abuse was my baby. We didn't know exactly what I was trying to do with it at first. But it became part of our journey. She has gone in a different direction but I am still here and she is still there if I need her. We had barely started the website in 2019 when April, Sexual Assault Awareness Month, came around. I always dream big so I had planned in my head to write and post every day. We knew that my strength was going to waver at times. Together, we made sure that my dreams of healing and supporting others were our main goal.

What is Dissociation and Why is it So Important to My Story?

 feel the description about dissociation in Complex-PTSD from Beauty after Bruises is the easiest to understand:

> *Interruptions in consciousness are prevalent – and at times a very scary – reality in Complex PTSD. Some may forget traumatic events (even if they knew of them once before), relive them intrusively, recall traumatic material in a different chronological order, or other distressing experiences of what is called dissociation. Dissociation is a symptom that exists on a spectrum, ranging anywhere from harmless daydreaming or temporarily "spacing out"; to more disruptive episodes of feeling disconnected from one's body or mental processes, not feeling real, or losing time; all the way to the most severe, which includes switching between self-states (or alters), as is seen in Dissociative Identity Disorder. Episodes of missing time can range anywhere from a few minutes, a couple days, or even large chunks of one's childhood. The larger gaps in time are typically only seen in DID, but those with C-PTSD alone can still endure "interruptions in consciousness" that result in memory gaps, poor recall, traumatic material that is completely inaccessible, or, conversely, re-experiencing trauma against their will (e.g. flashbacks, intrusive images, body memories, etc.).[1]*

As a general rule, the human brain is smart and adapts to what is happening around a person, knowing that we can only handle so much. Every day I play catch-up for conversations that are important to me. I need to remember to bring a journal to bed to write down these thoughts so in the morning I can read them to remind myself.

---

1 https://www.beautyafterbruises.org/what-is-cptsd April 7, 2021

The Evolution of Marc

How does one become a monster?

In 2017, the man who I thought would be my forever-partner changed, which made my mental health iffy at best. I was hiding in my bathtub at night. I constantly questioned whether it was worth fighting for my life anymore. I wasn't debating taking action to hurt myself, but I didn't want to take my medication and do the things to keep me alive. I was physically hurting and emotionally terrified. I couldn't figure out how I could have been so wrong about Marc.

Marc was the first person to see my dissociation. How could he cause things to be so much worse?

Marc and I met in the summer of 2010. I could write a book just on the ups and downs of our lives for the eight years we were together, but I'm going to stick to how he knew me better than I knew myself until things flipped on their head.

I remember our very first New Year's Eve together. We went to our friend's house and everyone was drinking and getting stoned. Many of the guys were getting handsy and grabbing me even though I only knew Marc and two others. I became overwhelmed and even though I didn't say anything, he saw it. He grabbed my hand and excused us from the party even though it wasn't midnight yet.

Marc then brought me home, talking and guiding me the entire time. He knew I felt more comfortable in the shower when I'm unable to speak. It's my safe place, but not necessarily with someone else. He helped get me mostly undressed; then took off only his shoes and stepped into the shower with me. For thirty minutes we just sat there together until I could communicate again.

It's always a little comical when I come back to center—I notice the silliest things. This time it was when I finally noticed he'd gotten into the shower fully dressed. It was not comfortable for him that's for sure, but for me it meant the world. I knew that even though I was in a compromised position he wouldn't hurt me. However, when I noticed I started laughing and said why did you wear all your clothes in? At which point he took his top off and tossed it in my face, with a laugh, asking, "Is that better?"

My memories of those moments with Marc are so crystal clear, the good years. Even though I struggled with C-PTSD some days he could see it coming and always supported me. We had fun and he was an amazing stepdad and later on biological dad. Pregnancy with my younger two was even harder than the first two, except at least this time I had specialists to work with. Marc was caring and supportive. When I'd cry in pain and want to give up because my entire body hurt and the vomiting wouldn't stop, he'd remind me how strong I was. I lived in the shower—the crazy-small stand-up shower in the small bathroom attached to our bedroom. He set it up with a folding beach chair so I didn't have to stand the whole time. This meant I would be sitting in the shower and he would stand half in and half out while he rubbed my back. He was my rock.

When I had my fourth child I had a massive clot. Luckily, the nurses noticed quickly and the doctors intervened and removed it. I was very weak and the doctors pushed me to have a type of tubal ligation or find a new doctor. So I agreed. After the surgery I became very anemic with severe pain for weeks out of the month. The doctors couldn't figure out what was going on but agreed that a partial hysterectomy was my best course of action.

In March 2017, I had a partial hysterectomy. When the day came for surgery, Marc and I said our goodbyes to the kids and headed to the hospital. He held my hand until I was wheeled into the back. When I woke up, my whole life changed. I was told my blood work was all over the place and I wasn't being allowed to go home till they made sure I was stable. So for a few days I sat in the hospital being poked, prodded, and tested to try to figure out what was going on. When I was sent home it was under direct orders to see my primary care doctors the next day.

I was then tested for numerous cancers and other chronic illnesses. We both changed. I felt like I was back at the beginning of my gastroparesis diagnosis, so I reacted in ways that worked before. I became more determined to fight through the pain in my body. Marc became afraid of losing me. His eyes lost the sparkle. He became mean, controlling, sexually and physically violent. He had a mental breakdown.

I say it was like two different people, but friends and family members will say that it wasn't quite as different as I remember. When we first met, he was totally disengaged from physical communication, instead retreating to video games immediately after leaving work. I used to make a joke saying, "If I was to walk in front of the TV screen completely nude, would you notice? Or just yell at me to move?" Once we had moved in together this improved for a while, but as soon as life got difficult, he retreated into his games. For me, this meant that no matter how sick or exhausted I was, I was still the main caregiver for four children.

Even though he was standoffish when it came to being a caregiver, he wanted control of what we were doing and more specifically when I ate and slept, etc. When we met, I needed him to take control and was okay with him not asking because, for the most part, I didn't know what I needed, other than someone to hold me. However, when he started needing to check my phone for texts, watch me shower, show him how much food I ate for dinner, and text or call the second I got to the YMCA and the second I was done with class, it became unbearable. I couldn't even remember what I had for dinner two hours after eating…

My brain had gone into dissociative (protective) mode. My mental health had plummeted. I was scared. I was stuck in fight-or-flight mode.

During the day, my routine was just a series of repetitive movements, which meant that I could do the daily tasks but I couldn't do anything new. I started getting upset calls from friends and doctors because I missed yet another appointment or birthday party.

Then night would happen.
I wanted to die.
I couldn't fight anymore.
I needed help.
I was afraid to ask my local friends and family.

Friends who I did reach out to said things like, "Husbands can't rape their wives; he would never do something like that, and he's so nice." I understand that it's hard to comprehend how someone's spouse could commit rape, but NO is NO!

Even now, I can still hear his words when I started exploring what Lifestyle/BDSM really is about…He shoved me face first into the bed and yanked my bottoms off. As he did that, he said, "You dirty little whore. I'll show you what dominant is." He held my face into the pillow, while I cried and said, "No." This was not what I wanted! This wasn't the first time he'd forced me but it was one of the most memorable.

Another memorable one would be the reason even the thought of anal sex still triggers me. The summer of 2017, we made my first trip back to Philadelphia to see the gastroenterologist who works with my gastric stimulator. The hotel we stayed at had a nice bourbon bar downstairs. I'm not a big drinker, but my favorites tend to be whiskeys or bourbons. There weren't many people there because it was a work night, so the bartender talked to us for a long time. When he found out why I was there he gave us free drinks, which meant I had two, officially one more than planned. I'm a lightweight no matter how much I weigh. I barely drink, and my stomach doesn't work, so there really isn't much food in it to absorb the alcohol before it goes to my blood. We made our way back up to the hotel room. The elevators make me nauseous even without alcohol. But this time I was literally holding myself up along the wall. Marc held my hand and pulled me down the hall to our room. Once we got in the room he shoved me face first into the bed. Yanked my bottoms off and before I knew it, I felt burning. With zero prep and no consent he decided to fuck my ass. When he finished I fell to the floor next to the bed and just stayed there in a ball. He got so mad. He kept telling me I wanted this. I didn't.

The last time I remember him fucking me was after he was discharged from the mental hospital. Not long after we had the following conversation I needed to talk to him. I was afraid of him! I didn't want him in the house. He wouldn't leave! We were sleeping in separate rooms, but he was unlocking doors and forcing himself on me. So standing six feet apart, I told him I was afraid of him. His response was, "I want to rip your clothes off and throw you on the bed."

I have very little memory of the next four months. But, luckily, this time I knew something was wrong. I needed out; I couldn't go back to this place! I deserved love and respect!

What do I mean by "I couldn't go back to this place"? Keep reading and we'll get there together.

One fateful evening in November of 2017, after baking cakes and going out with my sister, I received a call that would start me on the path to reclaiming myself. This guy called to talk about the birthday cakes I made. He didn't try to talk all sexual or want to ask me out. I wasn't in a place for that; I was still afraid. My husband was still living in my house even though we weren't sharing a room. I was afraid of him. At the time I wouldn't have said that but I had been retreating, slipping into survival mode. The last six months of my marriage were spent simply trying to get through each day since I couldn't remember the simplest of things anymore. Even with written schedules for each person in the house, phone alarms for doctor's appointments, alarms to remind me to pick up kids from school, I couldn't even remember what time my kids got out of school.

When I accepted this call, I had no idea that it would open up a world that would give me the control I had never had but desperately needed. However, first I needed to figure out how to get my husband out of the house. Marc would say he was leaving in two weeks and then change it to tomorrow and then next month. We finally got to the point that the four children needed to have a "normal Christmas." "Okay, I can do this," I told myself. "Just keep quiet, smile, and nod."

Staying quiet and nodding wasn't enough though. This man who I so desperately loved had become a monster and was using my previous traumas to keep me caged. I told him to leave one day and he grabbed my two younger children in a football hold on each side and said, "Fine! But you'll never see them again!" I blocked the door and tried calmly talking to him and reminding him that his children were petrified. The kids were crying, reaching out, yelling "Mommy!" over and over. I kept talking, saying anything and everything just to convince him to put our children down. That day it worked, but he wouldn't leave. We'd gotten through Christmas, but yet he still wouldn't go.

It was towards the end of January 2018 that he finally left. All it took was a little innocent picture that I would have taken months earlier if I had known it would stop my tormenter. I was sick; not contagious, just my body hating me. My youngest was still nursing, so she climbed up on the bed and snuggled in. I wasn't wearing anything, but had been mostly covered by the blankets. She was wearing one of my favorite dresses and her cloth diaper. While she was nursing I took a picture because I thought it was sweet. Well, she decided if there was going to be a picture taken she wanted Mommy uncovered and flipped the sheets down. I chuckled and sent one of the pictures to a friend of mine. Marc started screaming and when I wouldn't apologize, he packed his stuff and left.

He was finally gone, but the damage had been done. I was lost. Why couldn't I be happy? What had I done to keep being hurt?

Alone and scared, I needed to figure out how to heal. That's easier said than done, but, for me, finding a community that openly talked about consent and communication was a good step in my healing. So was getting trauma therapists.

In 2019, through encouragement from my trauma therapist, the blog started as a chronicle of my life, my experiences, and how I learned to deal with them. I couldn't fathom at the time just how much it would change me and heal me. My goal has always been that, in sharing my story, at least one person will feel less alone and have the strength to keep going. I've always wanted to help everyone else realize that they deserve to be loved and respected as they are. To me, that means opening myself up to exploring things I hadn't in the past, because they were looked at as evil according to others. When you stop thinking in the vanilla, the shades of gray and flavors of strawberry, chocolate, and everything in between open up, and fear doesn't control you anymore.

We should never stop learning and asking questions. [2]

---

[2] Adapted from athenatempestrose.com originally written February 12, 2019

What is This Place That I Can't Go Back To?

Hold on, I need to back up a few decades...like to birth

I was born early and given my last rites at about three months old, which I know because it's something that was talked about pretty much every birthday. My parents separated and later divorced without many memories of my father. Not long after that, my dad came into the picture. You may wonder why I say my dad came into the picture instead of a stepfather. When my parents got divorced my biological father signed his rights away to avoid child support, so my dad adopted my brother and me. In my house, there was a sign that said "Anyone can be a father, but it takes someone special to be a dad." We lived by that quote. As I got older I started questioning: Why wasn't I enough for my father? I was a child that needed my parents' love. Why couldn't I have that?

However, I did have my dad. And since I didn't really remember my biological father, I was pretty much okay with him not being there, at least until my mom and dad separated.

Was my early childhood bad? I don't think so? Just lots of moving for my parents' work. From the time my dad became part of our lives until I turned nine, we had what looked like a normal family: two kids, a mom, a dad, and cats. Yes, there were fights and holes in walls from my parents. But, I remember playing in hotel elevators, strawberry shortcake parties, trying to fly on my bicycle, baking snickerdoodles, and making mud pies. I have limited full memories; most are like snapshots in time or have been filled in by pictures or other people telling the story. However, I do have very distinct memories of a hurricane, a space shuttle, and my parents trying to "save" their marriage.

Hurricane Gloria ravaged the East Coast in 1985. Where we lived, she was a powerful storm, but what I remember is the eye of the hurricane. Honestly, I don't remember being scared at all. I do, however, recall the excitement and wonder when my dad walked my brother and me outside. I remember asking if the storm was over. He said no we're just in the middle of it. The sky was a brilliant blue and everything around was in this serene state. I didn't want to move a foot. Which was probably good, because the next thing out of my dad's mouth was, "Hold on to the railing, we don't want anyone blowing away." Of course, looking back as an adult, we weren't staying outside and waiting for the wind again.[3]

The second strong memory I have was from 1986, it was the day the space shuttle Challenger exploded. I had been to speech therapy that day so I wasn't sent back to school. At the time we had a sectional couch and a smallish four-season room. I don't know when, but my brother and I had arranged it into a square. I was set up to watch the space shuttle launch. As was strangely typical of me, I started jumping on the couch saying, "Blast Off! Then Kaboom!" My mom heard me once and came in to say, "Just 'Blast Off!' The shuttle is not going to explode." I just kept jumping until "Blast off!...Kaboom!" My mom looked at me and asked if I had recorded it and rewound it. Lady, I was barely six, and this was using videotapes, so recording wasn't super easy then. I accurately stated that the shuttle was going to explode. This was not the first time, and it wouldn't be the last, that I knew things before they happened. But for the most part my mother ingrained in me that it wasn't allowed.

---

3 We were just enjoying the beauty in the storm.

As my parents started fighting, which is what happened when my mother felt trapped, they had some very unique family days. I'm pretty sure this was some kind of last-ditch effort to stay together—they brought us to a nudist beach. My parents had a clothing optional policy when it was just us at home for as long as I could remember. Not something we talked about, but I knew they didn't sleep with clothes on and while they were in the upstairs it wasn't abnormal for someone to be walking around in just a towel or heading to the bathroom naked. When we arrived at the nudist beach it didn't seem very strange to me to see adults walking around with a towel and nothing else. However, when I got in the lake with my float and my bathing suit on...there was a problem. My float had a clear plastic section right at my face to look into the water. All I saw was penises. I'm not sure if that's where my dislike of seeing just people's penises or vaginas came from, but please either keep it covered or make it artistic.

Using counseling via sand play, I made my transition from the "real world" into my safe place. This is what I "saw" behind my house: my own private world. Complete with trees, animals, protectors, freedom to just be. It was not exactly how I pictured it because there wasn't every toy I could have wanted to use. It does, however, show what I was feeling. When you look head-on you see the backs of buildings leading forward to the front of my house. Just behind the house is greenery and the barn that blocks the visibility of what's behind it.

When I was around seven, my parents started fighting more than before. That's when things began to really change. They screamed at each other. Punched holes in walls. Drank a lot. Broke pans on walls. And tried to have my brother and I pick sides. If either of us questioned it even a little, the rage was turned toward us.

So, I would hide in my bedroom or out back on the overhang from the barn looking at the backyard. From the overhang, I would read and my imagination grew. The backyard became my own perfect Terabithia. Not too long ago in trauma therapy I was doing an exercise with sand and small toys. I was told to make anything I desired. I made my Terabithia.

I would climb up the tree or onto the roof of the barn and just read and daydream about the books I read. There are trees right after the bridge bringing you out of the city and into this magical place. Multiple animals needed safe homes but couldn't ask with words, so instead they found my little part of the world, which gives them safety.

With my escape into an imaginary land I also stopped sleeping very much because every time I would fall asleep I would have an awful recurring dream: the house would literally split in half. I would watch as all the rooms, toilets, sinks would fall away. Once the first split happened, first my dad and then my brother would start sliding and trying to grab onto anything to not fall. I would see my dad fall and then I would wake up. I started bringing a blanket and pillow into my brother's room and sleeping on his floor.

As the fighting got worse, my brother and I were sent to an aunt and uncle's house right after Christmas. We spent the week there—playing, going to work with my uncle, and just being kids. Then came time to pick us up. My mother came alone and told us they were getting separated. I was nine. That set in place a chain reaction that ultimately defined my childhood.

The Fallout Begins...

Forced to grow up at nine

As soon as my dad was gone, the house changed. My mother focused on work and friends. My brother and I were latchkey kids. Basically a ten-year-old (my brother) was taking care of me (a nine-year-old). I couldn't tell you when my mother was home and when she was not, but she usually hung out at a bar within walking distance of the house, so we would walk there in the afternoon to see if she was there and what the plans for dinner were. Since she was so relaxed about rules during the weekdays, you could be sure she was even less present on weekends, which are actually far more important in terms of being aware of what's going on in your own home. Once my dad was gone, my home fell apart. I started to be sexually assaulted and my mother knew nothing of it. I thought that was the worst thing that could happen to me. How was I to know this was just the tip of the iceberg?

My brother and I had always been allowed sleepovers with our neighbors whenever we wanted. However, not knowing the whereabouts of my mother allowed sleepovers at my house to become very different and scary for me. My bedroom was no longer safe. I can't tell the specifics of each event; they all blur together with no ability to know their chronological order. I started being sexually assaulted by another slightly older child. I think he was twelve when I was nine; he could have been around thirteen, but he wasn't an adult. Before I even understood what sex was, I hated the feelings in my body. Most of what I remember from those years is like snapshots from a camera looking over my body, but not actually

Reclaiming Me

living them. However, in all the snapshots, I don't remember my mother ever being around, even though it was her house.

There is one specific time I can recall but it may just be a combination of all the times put together in my head as one...

One night I was wearing a long nightgown to bed while my brother was having his usual weekend sleepover. Every weekend his best friend pretty much lived at our house. I had the smallest room in the house; it was so small that my twin metal daybed with a trundle could barely fit only one wall, with one dresser in the room on the other side. When you pulled the trundle out, the door couldn't be opened or closed and there was no floor space.

That night Calvin entered my room while I was sleeping and climbed on top of me. I woke up to him on top of me. I don't know what I said or did exactly at that point but I remember being confused. Calvin was always nice to me. He protected me from my brother's outbursts due to not having our dad while my mother tried to escape her demons through work and friends. My brother remembered our father, which I didn't due to being a year and a half younger. I just missed my dad so very much. However, I didn't miss the fighting, or holes in the walls.

Why was Calvin on top of me and why were his hands on my body? I screamed and one of his hands went to my mouth. He kept it there for a while till he could feel and hear my screams dying. I think he told me then to just be quiet and it would be quicker. He then started touching my body again. He was a lot taller than me even though I was not small at all for being at least two years younger than him.

While he was touching me in places no one had and tracing my skin I started squirming again, not daring to scream because I was still struggling to catch my breath from before. He once again took my hands in one of his and pinned them down against the metal frame of my bed. With his free hand he maneuvered his pants and underwear so that he was able to start sliding his penis along my underwear. That night I don't recall him actually inserting his penis into my vagina, just dry humping my clit on the outside of my underwear.

I wanted to scream again but there were no words coming out of my mouth. I was scared and all of a sudden my body was reacting in ways that I didn't understand. Why was there part of me that liked what he was doing? I didn't want him touching me and it hurt, but my body was also betraying me, making me feel something I never had before. Looking back now, I know that it was a physical response to sexual stimuli, but I didn't like it or agree to it at all. There are many science and psychology journals that discuss how this works. I find the following from Popular Science to be a good explanation:

> *Arousal during rape is an example of a physical response whether the mind's on board or not, like breathing.*
>
> *Adding to the issue is that sexual arousal and orgasm appear to originate from the autonomic nervous system—the same reflex-driven system that underlies heart rate, digestion, and perspiration. Our control over sexual arousal is no better than our control over the dilation of our pupils or how much we sweat. The presence of sexual arousal during rape is about as relevant to consent as any of these other responses. In violent assaults, intense physical arousal from fear can heighten sexual sensations in a process called "excitation transfer." In one laboratory study, anxiety from threat of electric shock enhanced male erectile responses to erotic images. The men in this study were not looking forward to the shock. They did not enjoy the shock. Their body's heightened state of physical arousal—anxiety about the threat of pain—heightened sexual arousal as well. Sexual arousal is just one more component of the fight-or-flight state.*[4]

---

[4] https://www.popsci.com/science/article/2013-05/science-arousal-during-rape/

After that first night he became even more like my protector during the day. Whenever anything was happening to me, he was there, whether it was my brother lashing out at me or someone making fun of me in a playground. The countless times I was my klutzy self, he was the first one to check on me. Calvin protected me. When I was at a younger age level in the church basketball league, he sat and watched my games. When my bra strap broke mid game and the coach wouldn't pull me, he caught the attention of a mom to force the coach to pull me from the game.

During the day, Calvin and his older brother (between fifteen and eighteen) would "watch" over me and either buy me whatever I wanted at the corner store or taught me how to steal it while one of them kept the cashier occupied. I learned quickly that being a white girl in a store with two black teens meant I could do just about anything I wanted. I hated the feeling of both stealing and knowing the cashier ignored me because of my skin color. His brother wouldn't touch me for payment. Instead, he had his own way of making sure I satisfied his needs. He had me kick him in the balls. At first, it was just in sneakers or barefoot, but after a while, he requested that I put on my mother's heels to kick him. I'm not sure how much the brother knew of what was going on with me and Calvin, but I believe he had to know something. Plus, I believe something was going on in their home.

During this time is when I started using what I now call survival mode or dissociative state. I functioned every day but wasn't actually making permanent cognitive memories. It hurt too much. My body was learning how to block out the trauma by separating myself from it, but it was too much, too often, to figure out how to turn back on.

It's funny and sad that while typing this in 2019 I realized the real reason I probably suck at geography of the United States. I probably was learning it in third to fifth grade—I honestly have no clue which one. I read my history and science books over and over again but I couldn't remember any of it. I could work on math problems and even reading because math doesn't require thought with me and reading because I escaped into the books and would finish one a day. Writing the report or taking a short test the following day didn't give me time to forget.

By the next day the book I had just read became blurred into my imaginary world, which I would escape to while bad things happened. In my head, as you passed into my backyard you would walk over a bridge into my version of Terabithia, which was an alien planet, complete with pegasuses, knights in armor, and centaurs that protected me, the princess. I lived in that world for almost three years—sitting on the roof of the awning attached to our barn or chilling in the big tree in our backyard. My backyard ran along a tree-lined division that would have connected four other houses on either our street or the street behind us. It was its own wonderland to me.

Where Were the Adults?

Why was I suddenly alone in a house with others...?

Now that my dad had moved out, my brother and I lived with only my mom. My mother just wasn't there at all. I don't know why but it was like she checked out of being a parent. I know that for a while she read electrical meters. At first, my brother and I would walk to a Portuguese family's house near our elementary school. It was nice to try some ethnic foods from my grandmother's side that I hadn't been exposed to because my father wasn't in the picture. The Portuguese family lived with their grandmother. She was the one to take care of everyone while their mom worked. Their mom seemed nice, but I only met her briefly. The two kids were a teen daughter and a son about my age. I looked up to the teenager and always wanted to play with her. Occasionally she would let me in her room to play with her and her barbies. I could tell she had outgrown them since they didn't move when I wasn't there. The time spent with them felt safe and happy. It didn't last long.

    I hear others talk clearly about things that happened to them in elementary school, but I honestly only have images and feelings to go on unless it's part of my journals or pictures. I have a vague memory/feeling that the reason we stopped being watched there is because my mom would call some afternoons and just direct them to have us "walk home," which we knew meant start walking towards the house and stop at the bar my mom's friend bartended at. I'm not even sure she had any idea how much time she was spending away from us.

Reclaiming Me

By the summer after my dad left, we no longer had an adult babysitter. Instead, she hired her friend's teen daughter. My mother was reading electrical meters and spending time with her friends or dating in her off time. That left a lot of time for my brother and I to spend alone or with a sitter. Our "sitter" was more just a warm body in the house. The first thing she would do when she got there was instruct us to go outside and play. Then she would call her friends and have them show up. They would go down to our basement and go through our food as well as our paper goods which were delivered monthly via a food service to save some money.

They literally took everything! I don't know who told me but I have a strong memory of being told that she had started feeding us our cat's food and calling it tuna. This may have been why my brother started trying to make "pancakes." These pancakes were literally the entire batter poured into a cast-iron skillet and placed in the oven. The first few were barely edible but over time they got pretty good. We even learned to put apples and other stuff at the bottom of the pan so when they cooked they would get all airy on top and on the bottom the fruit's juices would mingle with the sugar we put in and you'd have a fruit pancake.

The older kids in the neighborhood ended up bringing us to the park so we didn't have to stay with "the sitter." Instead, the city's recreation department had free activities all summer and even provided limited snacks and water. I remember getting lunch there, but I think someone just provided it for me in a brown bag. We didn't spend the whole day there, but something like nine to two. We played basketball, did arts and crafts, played on the playground, and occasionally went on field trips to places like Lincoln Woods.

In the afternoon, we had to go back to the house, where "the sitter" was still hanging out with her friends. One day I decided I wanted to rest and watch some TV. The only room other than the living room with a TV was my mom's. I have no idea why I was looking in her dresser, but I found her vibrator. Small barrel, beige nude color, lines on the plastic, two or three C batteries. The "sitter" walked in and found me playing with it. I asked her what it was. She said it was a massager for sore muscles and walked away. I probably spent an hour or so playing with it. For comparison, my kids found one when they were younger when a sitter was over. She told them it's an adult toy and to put it back.

My mom was struggling. She never wanted to be a single parent and even more than that, she didn't do well being single. She felt she needed a man to validate her being. Looking back, it was a revolving door of men, all of whom thought they would make good stepdads. However, my mother was hurting and didn't know what she wanted or needed. When I say revolving door, I mean there is no way I could list all the names of the males that came and went in my household. However, I do remember a few specific details. One had a canoe race that we went to. The race had my brother and I running through the woods to get over a bridge to the other side of the river. Another had a larger boat. He brought us to Point Judith. We got to swim off the boat. That was my first time on a boat larger than a canoe. Another supported my mom's softball playing, possibly playing himself? I don't remember much about him, just that he would go with us to the pizza place or restaurant after games.

As summer faded into fall, I turned ten, and sitters were no longer deemed necessary. We were supposed to be latchkey children. Too bad that memo wasn't shared with other parents on the street. Every day our house would be swarming with kids coming in and out as they wished. Except for Tuesdays and Thursdays. We had confirmation classes, youth groups, and basketball practices/games. Our pastor would pick us up each day and drive us over.

One day I really wanted a Skor bar, but they were all in the freezer. I didn't want it to be frozen. I had sensory issues, which weren't even a thing then, but nonetheless I had them. Skor bars are wrapped in aluminum. Do we see where this is going? Yup, I put it in the microwave. Snap, crackle, fire! I turn to grab a glass and fill it with water. Luckily, my brother was faster than me and ran outside to grab sand, which was already being thrown on it by the time I had a cup of water. He yelled at me, saying electrical fires cannot be put out with water and metal doesn't go in the microwave. I will never try either of those again. Thankfully, that was the only fire in three years of being left home alone.

It is Not All Dark

The positives that kept me going in the darkness

Those foggy memories contrast with a few amazing memories I have during that age range. Memories I will never forget, like getting a puppy, being able to watch and help her give birth to her puppies, spending time with my dad, and meeting Norm.

Everyone who has gotten a puppy knows what that's like—unconditional love but also chewed shoes and other craziness. Getting a new puppy is commonplace. Watching a dog give birth isn't, and was amazing. This was before the time of Google and cell phones so when she went into labor with only my brother, myself, and other kids in the neighborhood at my house, we leveraged all of our learning to help her. We found a box and towels to put them in and didn't let anyone other than my brother and me touch the puppies, which was only to be done when absolutely needed.

As the first puppy was born, Sheba, our dog, didn't know she had to eat the sac off the puppy to allow it to breathe. So I washed my hands and, as directed by the others, tore a small hole in the sac and pushed the puppy back towards Sheba. We all held our breath for a minute because someone had stated that dogs will eat their young if someone touches the animal. As we waited, she pulled the rest of the sac off, cleaned the puppy, and put it in the box. She then gave birth to seven more puppies and followed the same process.

After the birth we decided she needed quiet time so we brought everyone downstairs. Apparently she wanted us nearby, so once we got downstairs she started coming down one puppy at a time and was putting them on our couch. It was a pull-out sofa and very quickly one of the puppies fell in the space between the cushions and the bed frame. Sheba started panicking as we did too! Luckily, my brother was able to slide his hand in and, with help, gently maneuver the puppy through the metal pieces safely.

Thinking about Sheba makes me smile, but spending time with my dad was always a treat. He wasn't mad anymore. He got this two-bedroom apartment on the third floor, which felt more like an attic most days. It was either freezing cold or burning hot but we were happy when we were there. Heading to my dad's apartment from the house had my brother or me squished up against his side, holding the wheel and "driving." We would stop for a scratch ticket apiece and the special chocolate milk. During the summer nights, we would stay outside till late with the other kids and families. There was an empty lot next door and we all loved playing in it. As dusk would come, we threw balls and apples up into the air. Suddenly, the whole area was surrounded by bats. They were fun to watch most of the time. But remember that attic apartment? Well my dad's bathroom had a skylight for a window. One night when he went to use the bathroom in the dark, he found a bat swimming in his toilet.

On cold nights, the only real source of heat was the oven/heater and there were two bedrooms. My dad and brother shared the larger one with my dad having a queen-size bed and my brother having a twin on the other side of the door. My dad kept a space heater in there and closed my bedroom off unless I was sleeping over. When we got there after my dad's work, my door would be opened. Then, before I went to bed, he would take clay bricks, place them in the oven and then in my bed. Another thing my dad and I would do was work on our "secret handshake," which was more a hand clapping game than anything else and we would try to match each other and keep it going as long as possible.

Then came the best thing to happen in my life at that point in time: meeting Norm, my mother's boyfriend. I remember parts of that day clearly. We went to a local park and played on the brand new climbing structure. It was one of those pyramid rope things. By this point I had developed a slight fear of heights—probably developed from my repeated dreams of my house being split in two and my dad and brother falling out. I still loved going up, but coming down I started hyperventilating. Norm jumped up from where he was sitting and started talking to me as he climbed up to where I was. He then maneuvered himself around me so I knew I was safe as I climbed back down.

Not long after meeting Norm, he moved into our home. Norm would bring us to car shows, air shows, car races, hiking, and camping. One time, there was a solar eclipse and while the rest of the kids were trying to make cereal boxes safe for viewing the eclipse, I was sent to school with a welding mask. I felt super special and let all the other kids and the teacher look through for a minute.

The most embarrassing story with Norm was the day I got my period for the first time. I was in front of the entire fifth grade in my elementary school on stage during the annual spelling bee. I remember my teacher coming up behind me and wrapping her jacket around my waist and whispering in my ear, "When you are done, head to the nurse's office." I immediately spelled my next word wrong. There is no way I could tell you what it was, but I have a slight memory that on the way down the hall I yelled at myself because I knew the spelling. However, white pants and periods do not mix! Norm was the one who left work to come pick me up. He owned his own car restoration business, so he had more flexibility, and a phone in his office. My mother was reading meters and cell phones were still a thing of the future. He brought me home to change and then out to lunch.

Reclaiming Me

Afterwards, he asked me if I wanted to hang out at the shop for the rest of the afternoon or go back to school? I chose to go back to school. To this day I ask Why? It was one of the most embarrassing moments in all of my school experience. Back in the early 1990s, sexual education in my school was coed and started in fifth grade. As I walked back into my classroom all eyes were on me...then the teacher continued talking and put on a video. The video was in the same line as Look Who's Talking, a movie that came out a year or two earlier. When they mentioned a girl hitting puberty and getting her period the staring became laughing and pointing...

What I wouldn't have given to have just chosen to hang at the shop.

While Norm was there, I wasn't a burden. Instead, he played games with my brother and me. I remember afternoons of poker and blackjack, betting pennies and Kool-Aid cups. Those cups were coveted, so it was like winning big in a casino—I mean they changed colors! Most importantly, the assaults immediately started happening substantially less the second he moved into the house. He heard noises in the house and my mom became more present as well. She was happy and he was a good part of the reason.

The summer before sixth grade caused a bunch of changes for me again. My mom and Norm decided to move us to the house she grew up in because my grandparents were moving. I remember being upset at first that we were moving, but only because I was going to miss being the oldest in the elementary school and had earned my spot as a sixth-grade crossing guard, complete with my bright yellow sash. That quickly disappeared when I realized I was going to finally be able to be a kid again and go to sleep in my room without fear of being raped. So yes, moving was the best thing that could have happened, but the damage was already done.

However, that move also changed a bunch of things that I loved. We had been living in a diverse city. I played on the coed church basketball team. I was the center and one of the best three-point shots on the team. We moved to a small town where I couldn't even get on the middle school girls' basketball team because I wasn't friends with the girl whose mom coached. It didn't matter if I could play or not—I just wasn't given a chance.

We also moved states. For those who did not grow up in New England, you probably aren't aware there's somewhat of a hatred/dislike for the bordering states. We literally moved less than twenty miles away but teachers and students disliked me because I was one of "them."

Part of the reason we moved is because Rhode Island Credit Union screwed many out of their hard-earned money. Norm and his partner ended up having to close their shop together and parted on horrid terms as I remember. Over time he was able to build a business back up in our barn and garage.

For many years after we moved, I tried to remember exactly what happened during my childhood, even while still falling into survival mode repeatedly when bad things happened. I spent the first forty years of my life believing that these events alone were the ones that caused me to have such a warped sense of self-worth, but they were only a part of my trauma. The first event happened over thirty years ago and I can tell you that starting to write it out has allowed me to start processing the fear, pain, and confusion. Yes, for me, it's taken way too long! However, I can tell you that my body and brain are amazing in that they knew what to protect me from even when I had no idea what was going on around me. All children that have been sexually assaulted react in different ways. This is partly from their knowledge of the subject and others willingness to talk about these things. Calvin and his older brother probably have their own story to tell, because I believe no child learns these behaviors on their own.

Safe Spaces

How I made it through the bad times...

Moving was supposed to be to a new safe place. At first, I wasn't sure if my new home would feel safe or not. However, there were a small handful of places where I always felt safe. Camp and church were very important to me growing up. I knew I'd have food, adults watching over me, and feeling safe overall. Other safe places were at either my grandparents' house or an aunt and uncle's house. Finally, babysitting or volunteering at a nursing home made me feel safe.

When I went to pick up my older kids from camp in 2019, I remembered my safe spaces. There was always one positive to my story growing up and that was the time I spent at church and church camp. Camp, church, and spirituality have been important to me throughout childhood, my teen years, and now as an adult. As an adult my views have changed; however, my spiritual community is very important to me. That Friday, I picked up my older kids from church camp where they worked on Hairspray, Jr. What does that have to do with what I write about and what's important to me? So very much!

The show itself is about being open to new experiences and being one's self. This church camp is the same one I went to and adored as a child, adolescent, and teen. I met so many people there that have impacted my entire life. In the woods is where I felt safe and learned to be me. I tell a story occasionally about being a counselor when the new cabins were built. When I was first a camper we had these dilapidated red cabins. Have you

Reclaiming Me

watched the original Parent Trap? Think those but half the size with more kids in them. Well these new ones were so much nicer, but still with no toilet or showers in them. So one day, a fellow counselor and I needed showers...

I can't recall how we got away from campers and why we would have but something must have happened. So we grabbed our shower stuff and made our way to the bathhouse, which had continuous guests of frogs and various spiders. After showering one or both of us had forgotten some article of clothing, so we ran wrapped in towels to our respective cabins. I felt safer at the camp than I ever did in the real world.

This feeling of safety continues to this day, with my children following suit. There is no social media, cell phone access only for those who might need it, and wifi limited to places that need it, not for campers. The show isn't what caught my attention. It was the conversation after the show. Every year the campers and audience are told about what charity or purpose our donations are going to. This year was fresh on the heels of political drama, etc. The camp director got up and said his piece. He reminded us that the donations were for the campership fund, which allows the camp to open its doors to ALL!!! My base religion and camp are and have always been welcoming to everyone regardless of sexual orientation, gender identity, race, religion, socioeconomic background, etc...Yes, you must be respectful of all, but it is still a religious camp so if you don't believe in Jesus you need to sit quietly during songs and prayers if you do not want to participate.

Why am I writing about this camp? Well it's the first time in a while that I felt truly welcome. Yes, I still attend church and believe in Christ, but whether it's my divorce, my Lifestyle choices, my sexuality, or my desire for all to be welcome, I have always felt a little bit separated. That goes away the second I step foot in this sacred space. My life is full of good and bad memories but there isn't a single camp memory that is dominated by bad.

I can tell the story of getting stuck in the middle of the lake with another camper in a canoe and crying there until my brother paddled out with another counselor and jumped in, pulling us to safety. Or how about the story of me panicking at the top of the high ropes course? I stood there not able to move either way for twenty minutes till my brother was found. I was forty feet in the air with one rope over my head and one under my feet. The staff and other kids tried to convince me to just drop and I couldn't. However, once my brother was there, he told me to just breathe and step slowly. I got through it, and then the rest of the course...The zipline to get to the bottom may have been iffy too but still I did it and was so proud of myself at the end. My brother and friends and the staff of this camp would never knock someone when they are down. They lift each other up, focusing on strengths not weaknesses.

Camp was not the only place where I felt a spiritual presence that brought a feeling of love and safety. A few of my relatives' houses helped my sleep and overall well-being. My dad's father passed away when I was little but my grandmother was my world for a long period of time. Prior to moving to Massachusetts, I spent some time with her and she would cut up bananas in a bowl, put a teaspoon of sugar in, and then pour milk over it, or give me sugar wafers. She taught me how to play Whist and loved going out with just me. I didn't have to talk or explain how I felt when I was with her, just relax and be a child.

As I got older she became my escape whenever I needed. My cousins moved into her house and she moved into the in-law space that my Nana Brown (great-grandma) had lived in until she fell and broke her hip at ninety-nine. The women in my dad's family live long lives. My Nana Brown had a stroke when she broke her hip and could no longer do things on her own. For five years, my Gramma Rose had to help feed and clothe her in the nursing home. I think that was when she started saying that she just wanted to die peacefully in her sleep.

At some point in my high school years, she moved into an apartment near where my dad lived. When she moved there, she had a second bedroom so that way if I ever needed a place to stay, it was there. She paid for my high school, at least the parts that were not part of the financial aid I received. There were so many memories with her. I don't know how to pick out just a couple. However, the fact that I can easily pull those memories means that, as a general rule, when I was with her, I felt safe.

Mentioning Gramma Rose and all the good stuff she did brings back some of the memories with my mother that make me question if I have any worth in her eyes. Once my mom and dad separated, we were in a constant state of having no money in our house according to my mother. In middle and early high school, I babysat a lot and also worked with my mom removing wallpaper so she could prep a room for painting. As an eighth grader, I spent a month of Saturdays with my mother removing wallpaper to earn the leather jacket I was dying to have. I finally earned it the weekend of the Ross Perot campaign stop in Rhode Island. I was told the only way I was getting the jacket was if I went with my mom and Norm to the speech. I wasn't crazy enough to turn down what I had worked so hard for. It was loud and reminded me of rallies or protests I had seen on TV, but had not been allowed to go to for safety reasons. If rallies and protests were such a safety concern, then why was this one allowed? Because my mother wanted to impress Norm with all the things she could do with us.

When I was a freshman in high school, I had hidden and saved enough money to buy the car of my dreams to restore at home with Norm. I was beyond excited! I purchased a 1968 Camaro, four-door, with cowl induction hood, four-speed on the floor. I had a lot of work to do, but I knew I could do it.

When I say dream car, I mean I have a fictional story from high school where I wrote about racing the only other kid in school with a classic car. His was a 1969 Mustang, and the boy who had it came from money. He didn't have to work his ass off to afford the car or keep it running. If something on his went wrong they just called the mechanic and brought it in to be fixed. My story had us on the straightest drag in the area: Route 1. Might be straight but lights every hundred yards, whatever. We live in New England and there are no straight roads. So many jokes about that as an adult, but my dream was to race him right there. I knew how cars worked, how you shouldn't just slam the gas, and definitely don't jerk the clutch. However, on the other side Richie Rich just drove so, yes, I may have had an advantage. Since it was my story, I beat his ass, after allowing him to feel like he was going faster for about the first five seconds. He gunned it and tried to upshift so fast that he almost stalled it completely but instead just made the jerking motion that loses a race instantly. That was my story, now I had to actually live it.

Which meant, whenever I wasn't already working or going to school, I would be in the barn, working on the carburetor, cutting out the floor pan and welding in the new one, or getting the seats reupholstered. With Norm's help, I worked on the car as often as I could. I learned how to weld and cover dents with Bondo, then sand it down smoothly. I painted the inside of the trunk with special rust-proof paint and sealant and put the interior of the car back together with amazing leather seats, shiny steering wheel, a working AM/FM radio, working windows, and working heat. The car was ready for paint. I just needed to tape the stripes the next day before Norm would bring it to the spray room and paint it for me. I went to bed and the next morning I went off to school like usual.

However, upon coming home my Camaro was sitting on my front lawn for sale. I walked inside hysterical. I don't think I even took a breath before walking into the kitchen yelling about the fact that she had no right to sell MY CAR! My mother responded by saying we were broke and I wanted to continue going to my fancy school didn't I? Well, of course I did but this was my car and my money, it wasn't fair. My mother continued by saying it had already sold and the guy was just going home to grab a set of plates and have someone else drive him to pick it up. I was devastated but I didn't want to switch schools again so "Okay, if it's needed," I said.

As an adult, I spent a lot of time with my Gramma Rose. She was my world and supported me like no one else. It shouldn't have come as such a surprise to me that one day we were talking about how excited I was when I finally bought and fixed my Camaro. She asked me why I never drove it. I looked at her questioningly and said, "Well, my mom sold it to pay for my high school." It was her turn to look at me with confusion in her eyes. "I paid for your high school." "Wait! You what?!?"

Yes, my mom sold my car for her own benefit.

My mom's parents also had an open and welcoming home. My grampa was a lefty and loved baseball. I was also a lefty, so we bonded over things that right-handed people take for granted. He taught me how to throw a ball, peel fruit and vegetables, and tie my shoelaces. These things may sound simple and silly for me to remember, but to a lefty, just having one person around that works like you do is special. As I got older and really into sports I would call him to talk about the games I either had gone to or was planning on going to. As an adult I was able to bring him to a Red Sox game. We literally sat right behind the dugout. I have so many good memories of time spent with him.

My Gramma Easty (on my mom's side) is still alive and so amazing! Honestly, I cannot say how lucky I am to still have her in my life. Well, I'm lucky that I had so many relatives that, without knowing it, were saving me and protecting me throughout my childhood and teen years. Last year, I was finally able to talk to her about my childhood; it caused a whirlwind of emotions. I had been unable to drive for a few months because I broke my foot leaving her place one day and then I had to have my gastric stimulator implanted. Finally, allowed to drive again, I went to see my grandmother. When I arrived, she hadn't gotten dressed yet, but wanted to hear how I was doing. I had brought a grounding bag for her to see. I was taught to use grounding techniques by my trauma therapist. My therapist had stated she wanted to make specific grounding bags available for all trauma victims coming through the doors of police stations, ERs, and trauma centers. A grounding bag is for when I can't think or breathe. When the C-PTSD anxiety makes it so I'm not me and can't communicate. The bag can be used by either a person being triggered or someone witnessing the trigger. There are only three items in it, which, along with a couple exercises on how to help trauma victims, are located in the Appendix.

I'm not sure what I expected upon showing it to her, but it ended up being a long discussion about sexual assault. She needed to know why I made the grounding bags and then my history and writings. As we talked she never once questioned whether she believed me or not. Hearing what I had to say caused her pain, because she felt she failed me. She hadn't. It wasn't my grandmother's fault that I'd been hurt. She didn't live with me. She didn't know what was happening. Telling her now and hearing that she believed me no questions asked was that one thing I didn't know I needed so badly!!!

Why do I say it's the one thing I didn't know I needed? It gave me that confirmation that I wasn't crazy. She told me it wasn't my fault and I didn't deserve it. She was showing me that nothing that happened was my fault. It didn't matter what I wore, what I drank, or whether I originally wanted to have sex; the second I said no it should have stopped. She reminded me that I am strong. I am brave. I am powerful. I am loved.

Another very important piece that her belief, apology, and love helped me with, and I am sure helps others that have lived through assault and/or abuse, is the lifting of that weight and fear. "They won't believe my story." Why? Why is it so hard to believe a victim? First off, no one wants to believe a loved one is capable of despicable acts, which makes it hard for a victim to come forward. Second, the abusers have control, in public and out. They know the story to tell. They are nice and even-tempered and have already planted the story meticulously for people they come across. You and I, we who have been abused, can't even tell exactly what happened in order. We start at meeting the abuser, then jump all over the place because it hurts so bad to think about what happened. Some of us even black out or, like me, go into a type of survival mode so our body protects us from the pain.

So yes, my story seemed so off-the-wall to those I talked to at first! It wasn't until my closest friends and family could paste together what they had witnessed or heard or I texted that it all made sense. I lost at least six months of my marriage because my body already knew the skills to protect me. These are months he was able to tell his story while I struggled to even live. If someone tells you they have been assaulted, listen and believe; it's not something a person tends to lie about. Most people never report. The statistics are staggering and I believe they are still too low! Why do I say this? Because my story has gotten way more people sharing their stories with me, or just "thank yous", than anything else I've written. A handful of people simply respond with "I'm so sorry." These are the ones that know it's a problem but who haven't encountered it personally. Whereas many people responded with a "thank you for sharing. I've always felt so alone."

Now I'm Safe, Right?

New town...

If that was the case I wouldn't be writing a book, right? However, as I move forward the old fears creep in. "What if people don't believe me?" "What if people think I'm whining?" "What if someone who's had it worse reads my story and thinks I'm weak?" The thing we tend to forget is that pain is relative. Think of a baby that cries when they're hungry. To that baby, the pain of hunger is the worst pain they've ever experienced. A toddler trips and skins their knee, this is the worst pain they've ever known. As adults, many of us have felt that pain and we know how much worse it can be, but to those tiny humans, that pain is overwhelming.

Personal trauma is very similar; we all go through life on different paths, but that doesn't make your pain any less valid. We need to stop comparing ourselves to others as a way to belittle our emotions. That first heartbreak hurts the most. That first trauma will change you the most. But comparing your situation to mine is unfair to us both. We all learned to handle pain differently. While I learned to disassociate, others shove it deep; you may have learned to release it, and your neighbor may have learned to drink it away. This isn't to say that one way is right and the rest are wrong, they're just different. The way we learn to cope also affects our level of pain. Those who are able to deal with it immediately tend to suffer with it less, while those who try to pretend it never happened will let the pain fester like an infection until it takes over.

Over my life, many people have suggested writing as a way to help me process my emotions. A blog was never an idea I had but I did keep a journal at times. I think just the act of typing this all out, getting it out of my head, has helped me to see the different truths I've been fighting. I'm the type of person who lays in bed at night overthinking everything I've ever done or said. The ability to release those thoughts helps to quiet my mind. This is why a good portion of my writing is done in the middle of the night. It also helps me to look at it from an outside perspective. I'm able to see my needs that haven't been met, process pieces of my story, understand my emotions, and realize how my actions may have also hurt those I love. I'm also able to see the dominoes that have fallen because of how I responded to the things I couldn't control.

There are many writings that I've typed that I cannot consciously remember typing when I come back to edit. I read and reread as I let each piece fall back in place...Yes, it's scary! I've gone years where I thought I must be crazy. The only dissociations I knew about were like the story of Sybil and other psychological stories. And she hurt people! I don't do that so it can't be the same thing, right? Right, I do not have a personality that comes out with dissociation, it's more a lack of personality. It's a protective barrier.

What does dissociation look like in me? I do it to protect myself from the painful memories by allowing only a part of me to hold those. An example of my dissociation is I was extremely sick and in pain while I was pregnant with my son. At thirty-two weeks, prodromal labor started, and IVs were keeping me alive because of vomiting, which had caused me to lose fifteen pounds. It was excruciating and I remember crying and just wanting to die, begging for it to stop one night. But I only remember it as a one night thing and more as "Oh that happened," not that I cried like that every night for at least the last two weeks of my pregnancy, which I did.

To those of you who are reading this: I don't know your story, I don't know what you've been through up to this point, and I don't know where you are on your journey to healing. Regardless, I want to encourage you to write it down. I encourage you to release it from your mind and your heart, what you do with it after that is up to you. Burn it in a campfire, shred it in your office, turn it into a paper airplane and throw it off the tallest building. Whatever you do, allow yourself to release it and any pain that comes with it.

Allow yourself to heal.

Welcome to Middle School

In small town New England

The year is 1991, and we have moved to a new town not too far north. I have entered middle school, and I'm spending my weekends babysitting my younger cousins. They moved into my gramma's house and she is living in the in-law apartment, my own safe haven. Other than adjusting to a new district, the occasional bad teacher, and being one of the few kids in the school that believed race didn't matter in making friends it was a typical middle school existence most of the time.

Yes, middle school was relatively typical until you added in adult males wanting something to do with me. Examples of some of the not-so-typical times in middle school follow. It's been that way since I can remember. In the middle school cafeteria, in the hallways, and in math or health class, I got more attention than I wanted.

When I first started middle school I was super excited because the kids wanted to talk to me! I was one of the few that had been added to classes since kindergarten; small towns meant everyone knew each other and their parents. I was bright and shiny! I became "best friends" with the coolest boy in the class. We hung out at the elementary school behind my house and the woods there. My property was almost three acres and around it was the school, a factory with a large unused field, and woodlands/camps that went on for a few miles. He lived about two miles away on a dead-end street across from the woods. Looking back I can see the part of me that was also attracted to girls...why? Because as he talked and shared who he was attracted to, I would run through those girls' pluses and minuses with him. Awww, Makenna is gorgeous but a bitch. Ally is so sweet and yeah I can see why you like her, etc...

Till one day he decided he wanted my best friend. He asked me to give him her phone number. I told him no, because I got scared he'd decide she was more important to him than me. He got mad and I got mad...we both went home. The next day in the hallway he started yelling at me, calling me all sorts of names. I stood there frozen. Class had started and a teacher came out. I realized how much of an outsider I still was when she asked him what was going on. He responded with, "Athena's harassing me." She didn't even look at me, but told him, "Okay come into class. Athena, principal's office." Wait, what? Yup, small-town life...that city girl is trouble.

I went to the principal's office that day and was told to focus on my schoolwork. I was barely passing English and struggling in science. She said if I didn't show improvement in my grades and continued having issues with students I would be put on "in school" suspension or be forced to do summer school to move on to eighth grade. No mention of what had actually happened in the hallway.

I was only sent to the principal one other time in middle school. This one was far more interesting. I took the bus to school and home every day, due to where I lived. I was the first person on the bus and the last one off the bus. The bus driver gave me special consideration, which meant I was allowed to finish my breakfast on the bus and at the end of the day I would walk from the back of the bus to the front after the last drop off. Always done while the bus was moving. I was responsible for closing windows, picking up trash, and forgotten items. One day I was sitting in the second from the back seat and a boy behind me decided rather than throw his gum out he would just put it in my hair. When I got home my mom yelled at me then started working on removing it with peanut butter and Basic H. Most of the gum she got out but it hurt! She did cut a chunk out because it just wasn't worth the pain.

Flash forward a couple months and that obnoxious boy was showing off his brand new baseball cap. It ended up getting passed to me. I was asked to pass it back so I threw it "accidentally on purpose" out the window. A day later I was called down to the principal's office. When I got there my mother was already there. The principal quickly filled her in on what had happened and said I was accused of throwing it out the window on purpose. He was unaware of the gum incident and I had no desire to cause a he-said-she-said moment and just said, "Ooops! There is no way I could have done that on purpose. My aim is horrible." My mother agreed with me. At the time I thought she realized I was lying and just wasn't going to blow my cover. Years later I found out she believed that my aim wasn't that good. Apparently she didn't pay attention to any of my basketball games.

I've always been good at math, so much so that I was highest scorer on the school math team and John Hopkins University paid for me to take my SATs in seventh grade. That Saturday was literally one of the scariest days of my life. I was scheduled to take the test at a local city's high school because our town didn't have them that day. I had a cold and I was scared. I'd never stepped foot into this school before and now I was standing in it with hundreds of juniors and seniors. There were no separations for me from the high schoolers. I was sent to one of the cafeterias; luckily one nice kid directed me in the right direction. I sit down to do the test, and start sneezing. Snot is now running down my nose and I have no tissues. I can feel my face turning bright red. Just look down. Wipe your nose on the edge of your sweatshirt arm then roll it up. Focus! You need this! My mom constantly reminds me how smart my brother is, and then reminds me I can barely explain a book I "supposedly just read." Thanks, Mom. However, I did have this...just not enough to get the summer at John Hopkins. One question away in the English Language Arts section. The math was well above required. Both scores were higher than over half the graduating seniors in the country.

Moving before the start of middle school had given me some sense of being able to breathe easier, but that was just daytime. At night, I would sit up and talk on the phone to any of my friends that were willing to. At the time long distance cost money for every minute you were on and there was only one line in the house. I was lucky enough to have one of those clear phones with the neon insides in my bedroom, but almost I lost it a few times because of the expensive phone bills. I had become terrified of sleeping in my bed alone.

I had started a pattern of needing someone to "keep me safe" at night in my house before we moved. On the nights my brother's friend wasn't over I would grab my blankie and teddy bear after my mom went to sleep or to her room, and lay it on my brother's floor. It was the one place in the house I felt truly safe. Some may ask how I could feel safe with him since I also say he would get angry and hit me. I knew all along he was only hitting me because I was the only one that was there. He is my big brother and loves me, but was struggling trying to find his place as well. Why did everyone leave us?

My brother and I pretty much did anything we wanted because our mother just didn't pay attention. Basically, don't talk back or say anything rude to Norm and you stayed under the radar unless she was having a bad day. This meant she didn't even think twice when we had other kids over for coed sleepovers or we would also go to other camp friends' houses for the same type of anything goes party.

At one of these parties I think I had my first kiss. Or it could have just been a kiss that is memorable for all the wrong reasons. We always played truth or dare at the parties. This one was the only one at Jennie's house; her parents allowed us to use their "cabin," which had multiple bunk beds built into the walls and a large living room area. So, Matt had been given the dare to kiss me. He came over and shoved his tongue in my mouth. All I tasted was Doritos! Yuck! Not what you want when you are kissing someone. So me being me, I spit right into his face. Oops!

Another one that happened at our house was the final summer of my brother living with us. We set up a ten-person tent in the backyard facing the pool. You couldn't see anything we were doing from the house. We even had a bonfire going. We played truth or dare and hide-and-seek on the school and factory grounds. I had my "first boyfriend" there as well and we made out. We kissed and went to second base—have the bases changed since I was a teenager? As adults we chuckle a little when someone tries to talk about sex in terms of bases, but I still think it's kinda cute.

After the party my brother and I were picked up by our dad and spent the night in a hotel. You could tell just how little I had slept the night before because I passed out as soon as we got into the room. I remember my dad waking me up to tell me he would be outside because the fire alarm was going off. He had already walked out of the room once to check what was happening. He also stated it was likely pulled by someone in the middle school/high school group that was also staying in the hotel. So he said I didn't have to leave; but once I was awake I was shaking and couldn't figure out how I had been sleeping through such a loud alarm. I don't like breaking rules, it makes me very anxious, so I put clothes on and walked outside with him. After that night, I was brought home and my brother went home with my dad. My dad was living in Delaware at the time so he went and moved there. I was able to visit once but that was it. After that I was for the most part an only child.

Once my brother was gone the only way I could sleep was on

the phone. If I couldn't call anyone I would go outside in the late spring through early fall and take a pool float out and lie on it in the middle of our aboveground pool. No one could touch me in the pool...until the twelve-year-old me met the twenty-two-year-old tenant on our third floor. In my head I've always remembered what comes next as a high school thing. This is because I couldn't process meeting an adult at thirteen or younger that I would somehow have a sexual relationship with. I did though, because he was a predator and knew exactly what to do to entice me and keep the adults from even questioning what was happening.

I met him going into seventh grade. I was about to turn thirteen when we met, which would put him turning twenty-three. Our birthdays were both in September. We met briefly in the spring of sixth grade. One night not long into the summer season, after Whitey moved in, he was at the pool when I snuck out after bedtime. He just talked to me at first, then every night he would meet me outside to "keep me safe."

That summer and the fall of seventh grade had me just running around babysitting and living what I thought was a normal middle school life. Along with camp and church I just enjoyed what I thought I had. One of the most fun things during that time was Rev. He was one of my first "boyfriends." We were camp friends and pretty much all of us dated others. He lived about thirty to forty-five minutes away, so not super close, but my cousin never had a problem picking him up to come hang out with us when we did fun things.

My favorite outing with him was to Rocky Point. If you don't know what it was and still is now you should search it. We all loved Rocky Point. At the time it was still fully functional and I think my dad may have been working in the office there at that point. So my cousin picked him up in her Ford Bronco. There were not enough seats in the car for all of us to be properly buckled but at the time it didn't matter. The two of us jumped in the trunk and had a bunch of private space to do what kids do. Yes we definitely made out and sang to the music my cousin was playing. Our song was Boys II Men's "End of the Road," so when it came on we happily belted it out. The summer of seventh grade was probably my most normal summer. Even though Rev and I have long since broken up, we continue to remain close. As is the case for many of my camp friends, we may not see each other for years but the second someone needs something we step up.

During my final year of middle school I had a good amount of things happening. First, my male friends were starting to become interested in girls and I had very few female friends in that small town. All the kids had gone to one of two elementary schools so they all knew each other when I moved in starting sixth grade. At first it was okay because they wanted to know all about how a diverse city school was compared to theirs. The most embarrassing middle school incident happened in the school cafeteria. I was one of those girls that developed breasts early. By eighth grade, I was wearing a DD cup. One day in the cafeteria, a group of boys came up to my table and sat down. This in itself wasn't super abnormal since I tended to hang out with the boys, but today it was different. One boy sat uncomfortably close to my side and before I knew what was happening he had poked my breast with an open safety pin. First one then the other to be sure; they were looking for my boobs to pop like balloons. Finally, I managed to cover my chest and had the majority of the grade staring at me laughing. I was mortified and not one teacher even noticed or came to my aid. I never wore formfitting clothes for the rest of middle school. Baggy clothes and head down for the rest of my time there was how it would go.

After that I mainly kept my head down and chose to focus on the classes I was good at and spent recess/lunch breaks in the math teacher's room. But even that teacher was treating me differently than other children. Why was I different?

Reclaiming Me

I don't really know, but this is how teachers treated me. One would expect my math teachers to at least notice me, right? Yes, because it's really easy for me. But this seems a little over-the-top right? A typical conversation with my teacher: "Hey sweetie can you stay after school today to tutor Johnny on this since I've noticed you have your own way of working through a problem?" "Okay, Mr. Pie." At the end of the day when the other kids went home, I would walk into the classroom with my backpack and stuff to go home. Students would come in and I'd be told to start with Monday's lesson and explain how FOIL worked and how to find the x, y coordinates. He would watch me intently. Then when the kids seemed to get the work he'd have them work together for a bit, while he called me over to his side. "Amazing job today," he'd say as he brushed my leg with his hand just below desk level so those on the other side didn't see it. At the time I didn't think twice, but looking back that's not acceptable.

I still don't know the true answer to why I was treated differently. So you can imagine I had no idea what made me different at twelve and thirteen. I can tell you now that there were differences between me and the other kids. One was that I had moved a lot before middle school, so no one else really knew me. Another was that my parents were divorced. I had been sexually assaulted for three years before even moving to the small town. The biggest difference between myself and the other kids in my grade was that I knew more about adult things because my mother didn't hide those things, but she also didn't try to help me understand them. There was never anyone there for just me, until Whitey entered the equation.

When school let out for the summer I started my own "babysitters camp." I didn't know what to call it, but I loved The Baby-Sitters Club and babysitting so it just made sense. I was also already babysitting for multiple families on different days; this sounded even better. For a few weeks that summer I had six kids that I was watching. They came either having eaten breakfast or carrying it with them. We played in the pool or sprinklers. Did some yard games and board games, mostly when it was raining. Watched a movie occasionally. I made lunch and snacks each day. We tie-dyed shirts, colored each other's hair with Crayola markers (they came out with shampoo), made up our own sidewalk games, and had a creative discipline system.

As a child, how do you discipline other children? It's difficult. I mean it's difficult to discipline my own kids sometimes. As a group we decided that the super soakers were a way to remind the child that wasn't doing as told to focus. At first the kids would just push limits so they could get wet. That was until I switched it up: if no one got sprayed all day they could all get a bucket, balloons, hose, or super soaker and let me have it. The first time they won they had so much fun drenching me. It became a push within the group to be good just so we could have a water war. The only other time I remember them winning was a day Whitey came home at the perfect time. The kids decided it would be fun to soak him. I helped set it all up and when he got out of his car all hell broke loose. There was laughter from all the kids and myself...but I could feel he was pissed!

I knew I was going to be in trouble when he looked at me. However, it left me with a very happy feeling—it meant I was being noticed! Did I care that he might hit me, not let me watch TV, or sit by myself on the couch? Not at all! As long as he would let me be near him I didn't care! However, those first few months, possibly years, he didn't use corporal punishment. I wanted to make him happy so I tended not to push limits and after that first super soaker event I never did that again! At thirteen, he was the only Daddy figure just for me. He instructed me on clothing, hair, food, bathing, and protected me from my mother and others that were only out to hurt me. He noticed when I woke in the morning and when I went to sleep. He knew my habits better than I did.

Reclaiming Me

That summer we only spent time in and around the pool. At first he would just come over and talk to me while I stood outside. Then slowly he started hugging me. This continued to the point where he would come over to me and start massaging my shoulders, and then gently slide his hands down to my breasts. This was the first time I wanted a male touching me. The heat between our bodies steamed along with the pool water at that time of night. When I questioned my self-worth he would tell me I was beautiful and deserved more. More attention, more love, and more protection. I told him that summer all about my history. He wanted me to talk and it made me feel safe. Whether in the pool or by the cars just walking by each other, he made sure to touch my skin. The electricity it caused in my body was like lightning up and down and this was just a simple brushing over my hand! In the pool I felt as though I would die if he let go. I kept urging him in my head to run his hands lower, my breasts were not enough, but for that summer, night after night he always stopped right there. He would pull me in close in his swimsuit and the back of my body would curve to his front, but his hands would never touch anything but my shoulders and breasts.

As the summer continued, I was babysitting the renters on the second floor of my house and pretty much spending all my time up there even when the kids' mom was home. She and her husband were fully aware of the relationship that was developing with Whitey. They would let me sneak upstairs to see him or to sit on the stairs with him while I was at their apartment.

When school started the pool quickly became too cold to meet at. So he distanced himself. Told me I should get a middle school boyfriend. I reminded him I did have one from camp. The statements back were ones of, "You're a little whore just running off and screwing anyone. See, you don't care about me or you wouldn't be dating." However, on the other side, he was dating and replied with, "I'm only dating her so no one tries to take you away."

I spent the rest of the year trying to seem like a regular middle schooler, but my ability to retain information was severely lacking. I couldn't remember my own name. Reciting the Gettysburg Address was impossible. At the time I had no idea what dissociation was; looking back I can tell you I lived in that state for a better part of the ten years I knew Whitey.

At some point, towards the end of eighth grade, I was moved from the first-floor bedroom that was bright and clean to one of the two bedrooms in the basement. The nicer room became my stepfather's office and his computer room because it had a phone line in it and he didn't like the darkness of the basement. He flew helicopters for the army reserves and was always practicing flying when he wasn't working on cars. This was just one of the times where it was painfully obvious that others came before my brother and I in my mother's eyes.

I almost made it through the rest of middle school blending in…that is until the weekend before school let out for the summer. I had a sleepover for my school friends. We had fun, made pizza and snickerdoodles, played truth or dare, and then got ready to "sleep." As we were getting ready a large pair of nude colored "granny panties" was found. Immediately, everyone said they were mine and started laughing. I screamed, "They aren't mine!" Everyone else said, "They aren't mine either," "You're fat," and, "This is your house so they must be yours." I tried saying they could be my mom's. No one cared. I knew they weren't mine or my mom's. I actually had a pretty good idea whose underwear they were, but I preferred being the one made fun of over throwing someone else under the bus. I didn't go back to the school, knowing that come September most of those kids I would never see again as I was going to a private Catholic school for high school.

Changing the Narrative

My thoughts are not my own

Whitey was building his narrative to consume my free will. It's not something that happens overnight. Middle school was the time he showed that "he was sweet and caring." He would nod when we walked by each other in the hallway. He was "protecting me from being sent away by my mother." Yes, those were his words. If my mom found out I was talking to him, he said I would be forced to live somewhere else. It would be all my fault if *he* got into trouble. So whenever I saw him outside or in the hallway I pretty much was told to pretend I didn't know him.

I'm writing this at the age of forty-two after only realizing in the last few months that I was groomed by a man while I was a child. The people that were supposed to protect me did not. My ability to understand and feel what love is supposed to look like is so skewed by this fact. I am perfectly capable of showing others love, protecting them, and raising them up...but how do I change the way I see myself? The hope is that by writing out how things were I can process the truths and see how skewed my perception is.

> *'Grooming is a process by which offenders gradually draw victims into a sexual relationship and maintain that relationship in secrecy. At the same time, offenders may also fill roles within the victims' families that make them trusted and valued family friends.* [5]

---

[5] Copied from the Red Flags of Grooming; March 7, 2022; https://www.d2l.org/

I'm going to try to explain what my grooming looked like to help you understand. I didn't even quite grasp just how effective and dangerous grooming was until I was focusing on writing out my experiences. Which is why I don't expect someone who hasn't lived through grooming to understand fully. Depending on which website you click on from your Google search you will get slightly different detailed descriptions that explain grooming as a process that changes the victim's perspective of things around them based on the abuser's wants. Grooming is very different from Stockholm Syndrome because you never feel like you were captured even in the beginning. Instead you go to the person out of what feels like being loved and cared for. It works easiest on children that already have a traumatic history. It is subtle at first; you don't see what is happening, the perpetrator controls the narrative.

I actually have no clue how to start this…It all seems so foreign to have a choice. To be the one deciding what happens next. Not to have to ask permission. Even now where I live my dad controls what I'm allowed to eat or do in the house. I try to escape most weekends because it means I can write and date without being treated like a nine-year-old. He won't help with the overwhelming kid schedules, or their mental health stuff, or driving, but yells at me for not doing enough. He doesn't accept that I am disabled even though he watched me almost die multiple times. I don't understand. When I was sick at seventeen he stayed with me—he literally had bought a new place and brought me over. Well I christened it with multicolored stomach acid. Fifteen years ago when I was just being diagnosed with gastroparesis he would come to my house every day. He would clean and make sure I had food even though I barely ate and got sick immediately after. Why does he not believe me now and hate me so much? All this means every time I try to write with him home I get anxious and nothing comes out.

---

the-red-flags-of-grooming-behavior/

I have been struggling writing my story with Whitey so much! He took my childhood in ways that can't be explained, because they never happened. I wasn't allowed to make mistakes or hang out with friends drinking or just having sleepovers. The few sleepovers I was allowed were those at my house where he could watch through the window if he desired. For over three years I've kept trying in vain to just put it down on the page. However, I figured I'd try writing this piece of my life tonight because it was a different environment: a bar tied in rope. I decided to start typing and what do you know, my brain works. Loud ass music and lights...no distractions I guess?

Whitey had already started controlling me well before I started high school. I had a big glowing target on me: I was the twelve-year-old hiding by a pool at night alone. We lived in the same house, so he definitely heard the yelling, and since my room was level with the driveway and right next to where he parked it didn't take a lot to connect the dots. I can't tell you when I first met him or how long he had been living in the house before he decided to show up at the pool that first night. But he was definitely watching me and making mental notes.

While he was watching me he was also talking and becoming indispensable to my mother. She would stop him anytime he came home in the hallway and talk about the pains in her body and get his "expert" opinion (he is a paramedic and firefighter). This would put her mind at ease, and quite often contradicted the doctors. While they were talking, I would come home from school, have a towel on after a shower or various other reasons to be walking around our house in less than presentable attire. Both of them would always notice me. She would outright tell me to get to my room and cover myself. He on the other hand would look at me as if I belonged to him already. If I saw him without my mother he would say how beautiful I was and that my mother was just jealous.

Reclaiming Me

By the time Whitey ended up at the pool that night, he knew I was basically alone and needed someone to just notice me. Once that first night at the pool happened it was like a vault had opened and I started sharing my life. He just listened even though many pieces were just filling in small blanks. Those nights by the pool allowed him to get to know all my insecurities. He needed to know why I didn't sleep well. This became his reason for inviting me up to see him every night he didn't work. As the seasons changed he started to invite me upstairs to watch old movies. Over the course of two or three years we watched Casablanca, every Charlie Chaplin movie, Red Green Show, and The Three Stooges along with many others. I was sleeping in his bed every night he was home, until waking up at quarter to five in the morning to sneak back down the stairs and into my room which luckily was just off the hallway for now.

I badly needed someone, a Daddy, to protect me. A male that wouldn't leave me either alone or alone with my mother. I would have given anything for my biological father, my adoptive dad, or my stepfather to take me out of that house and just hang out. I probably shouldn't say that about my stepdad, but he, like every male I've noticed around my mother, becomes different from what they were at the beginning.

Even though I grew up Methodist/Christian, I've been realizing that there are so many things that we can do to affect the way the world is around us. My family also has a lineage tie to Salem, Massachusetts which has caused my interest in metaphysical exploration. I've recently been pondering the thought of a family line spell to attract people to us. Is that even possible? And why would anyone, but it's truly the best description I could possibly come up with for why the revolving door, why all my aunts were married (even those that were widowed), and why my children and I never seem to have a lack of opportunities for partners but not necessarily the ones we need.

The move had left me feeling very alone. My mom was happily focused on making the house hers. She was happy with my stepdad and helping him restart his business. My brother was very mad we moved away from his friends. Luckily for him he is an extrovert and made friends easily. Which meant during school he did great, but home was different...

He remembered things I didn't, which meant he was hurting. When I was twelve, my mother was already kicking my brother, who was only thirteen, out of the house. She said he wanted to leave and wouldn't abide by her rules. But I needed my brother. Which meant anytime I mentioned it she would yell at me saying, "You know your brother forced me to kick him out so he could live with your dad. Stop feeling sorry for him!!!"

In the move to small-town life my mom went back to wallpapering and painting for herself. In seventh grade I really wanted a leather jacket, which all my friends had. I don't know why I didn't use my babysitting money to buy it but I didn't. Instead she made me go on weekends with her and Norm to peel wallpaper and prep for paint. I earned that leather jacket and then some.

The day where she deemed I'd earned the jacket was also a rally for Ross Perot. My mom and Norm were all about voting for him so they made me go to the rally. Everything in me just wanted to run. I didn't do well around that many people and also had already started avoiding political topics in my family as everyone was very strong-willed and were always getting into fights about their beliefs. However, I did make it through and was in awe about how Mr. Perot inspired the entire audience to action. This man was the first independent since 1912 to actually affect the presidential vote. He received 18.9 percent of the popular vote. Some have said that he was the reason President Bush did not get a second term, but there is no data to prove that statement. In fact, those that voted for Perot were split between both parties, according to exit polls.

Reclaiming Me

My mom and Norm got married when I was in eighth grade. I was so excited to have Norm in my life! I remember helping him plan popping the question. Every morning my mother would make Norm his lunch: a peanut butter, jelly, and Fluff double-decker (three pieces of bread, one sandwich). So the night before he got the bread out and cut a hole in a few pieces of bread right below the top one. There was no way my mom would miss the box. It was her birthday. We all needed to get moving, so he asked her to make his lunch so I could get on the bus and he could get to work. She stared at him in disbelief. "You aren't taking me out for lunch on my birthday?" was her response. So I looked at her and said, "Can I please have a sandwich for lunch?" To which she looked at me quizzically. I barely ate sandwiches as such. Usually I just grabbed the parts and put them in separate baggies. She grudgingly grabbed the bread and said, "What do you want?" I looked at her and was like, "Peanut butter and Fluff?" She was so mad! I never ate that. "Really?" she said. "Yup!" I replied. With a shake of her head and a, "Fine," she opened the bread finally. Norm got down on one knee and she finally saw the box. She said, "Yes." And then there was some laughter and pissy comments back and forth. Ending with her finally asking me if I really wanted that sandwich. "Nope," I said as I grabbed my bag and ran out the front door for the bus.

The proposal happened in October. The wedding was planned for April, taking place exclusively in our yard. I believe my brother was living with us at this time but I honestly have no idea—this is what complex PTSD looks like (breaks in story lines, confusion of details, knowing the bigger picture but unable to seamlessly piece it together). My family is full of amazing bakers. My great uncle even worked for the Kennedys for a period of time, so clearly we would be making our own cake and my mother decided on chocolates for favors. I was responsible for helping her make about six hundred each white chocolate, milk chocolate, and dark chocolate hearts. It's highly likely that by the end of the making

I was doing it all on my own. She had to start on other pieces. Whitey was very displeased that I was spending all my time in my kitchen helping prep for the wedding, even getting to help with the cake and having my uncle, whom I adored, buying quarts of strawberries every day just for me. He literally was hiding them from everyone else. It made me feel special. He didn't say a single word about my weight; he always said I was beautiful, intelligent, and capable of doing anything I put my mind to.

Alone and unheard is the way that Whitey needed me to be so he was not pleased when my other relatives were around. I didn't realize this at all so I still happily bounded up the stairs in the evening to hang out, but so many nights he pretended not to hear me. I felt like a lost puppy just trying to make my owner happy but I was instead ignored. So I threw myself into the wedding planning and I had to work on my singing. My mother and Norm had asked me to sing "(Everything I Do) I Do It for You" by Bryan Adams during the ceremony. I was shaking.

My mother has a need for everything to appear perfect to others when they are entering our home. This means that everyone gets put on edge and there is yelling more and more until the time of a party. I was responsible for mowing the yard before the tent went up. Luckily the wedding was planned for the end of school's April vacation. It was a gorgeous week so mowing was fun. We had a tractor, which I loved driving with my headphones in and a mixtape on. The Reverend came over and we ran through the rehearsal then went out to dinner the night before the wedding.

There was drinking…Tempers flared at dinner so by the time we got home I just hid in my room till the next morning. My mother was mad the weather had not cooperated at all. It was rainy and raw! Luckily we had the tent but we needed to grab some space heaters and the weather protectors for the sides. The house was pure chaos. People pushing and shoving everywhere. I was overwhelmed and just wanted to hide, but that wasn't allowed. I was yelled at to finish prepping the favors, move this, and take out that. It's just how life was when my mother needed something: she delegates and yells. Life is not fun in these moments but we always get through it. I always knew anything I put my mind to, it would happen. However, I didn't know how to make it beneficial because bad stuff was always happening and that's what stuck in my head. I was worthless and therefore deserved to be alone and punished.

That horribly rainy day in April was no different. All the guests arrived and were warm and happy inside the tent. I got my dress on then helped my mother put hers on. All the while she kept grabbing the top of my dress and pushing my boobs down into it. It hurt and I wanted to cry but I knew better. She told me again that I needed to lose weight and to stop trying to showcase my boobs. My boobs were ugly and a reminder of my father's family. As usual she led with, "You're your father's daughter and you need to lose weight and dress appropriately. That's why the boys keep looking at you. They think you're a slut and ugly." I ran off in tears but knew I better be back in time to apologize and join the wedding party. So I just sat off behind the barn where no one could really see me. Except of course Whitey found me. He told me I looked amazing in the dress but needed to put on a sweater over it because it was cold and he didn't like other men looking at my boobs. I smiled through the tears and got up to find a cardigan for him.

The rest of the evening went amazing. My mother was happily drinking and having fun with her friends. Norm was hanging with me and his friends. We were all just dancing and singing. My favorite song was "Another One Bites the Dust," because Norm jumped up and sang it at the top of his lungs. I'm not sure when I saw Whitey again that night but he motioned me to come over to him. So I did…and was told to get inside and put warmer clothes on. I was not to be outside with "grown ass adults staring at me." I listened because it meant he cared.

After their wedding, I started withdrawing from other kids

because Whitey told me he needed me. Did he really? Nope, it was just so he could isolate and control me. One of the ways Whitey isolated me was by requiring me to spend nights with him as well as dressing to minimize my curves. I've been complimented by strangers based on my facial structure, breasts, and booty since I can remember, but my mother and others close to me always said I was fat and ugly. I saw Whitey after a day of summer work-study, which is required for those on scholarships. He asked me how it went. I told him about my conversation with one of the teachers. I wasn't surprised when he flat-out told me that when school started I was not allowed to wear my school skirt. Even worse he told me t-shirts were required under my button-down shirt. I did as I was told because I trusted him, thought he was trying to protect me, and thought it was so no one would make fun of me.

As I've stated, I was excited when eighth grade ended knowing the next year would bring a different group of kids in a new school. The perfect time to rewrite who I was. Summer started with some sneaking upstairs but mainly lots of packing. I was spending weeks at camp—literally my mom signed me up for every camp our church would pay for. I loved it there. I had friends and adults that I respected and they all taught Love above all else. We were the "in" crowd, but really as long as you talked you became part of the cool kids. It was a rainy summer, which did stink for camp because it limited campfires and time spent outside doing rope courses and various games, but we still had a great summer.

During summer camp that year I became a Counselor in Training. CIT was always run by the camp director. His booming presence always left me grounded. He made camp. We all knew what to expect. I don't think I ever heard him falter, not that he didn't have fears, but he didn't let us see them. All we knew of him was his love for camp and all of those in it. This also came across as a known boundaries type thing. We knew the rules and consequences—always a little afraid of them but I'm not sure I saw them enacted.

As summer ended, my mother saw its effect on my hair and made fun of me. Due to the weather and my stomach I hadn't spent as much time outside as previous years. In the past I would have just said the weather was the issue, but honestly my stomach also played a huge role in whether I was outside or not. Stomach disabilities are not things most people talk about. It actually seems even more taboo than talking about sex. However, it's important and has impacted my life pretty much from the start. I was a premature baby so it would make sense that my digestive tract might have had issues upon birth but it was never talked about, no matter how much I cried in pain. Well, until my mom had to have her gallbladder out when I was a freshman in high school. Then we talked about her pain. Since I've pretty much put forward all the embarrassing and not quite so embarrassing aspects of my childhood I might as well add this one in. Due to being a premature baby I had some things that never quite seemed right, or at least that's the easiest reasoning to go with.

As a kindergartener, I vividly remember one very snowy day where all the kids were down the street hanging out behind the convenience store since the plow had left an eight foot bank of snow. I wasn't allowed to go when everyone else did because my dad had given me a suppository. I hadn't gone to the bathroom in probably a week, which became the norm as I grew up. Suppository done, I sat and waited, and waited...till over an hour later when my dad finally said just go play, apparently this isn't going to work. He helped me get my snowsuit on. I ran down the street and started playing with everyone else...when all of a sudden my stomach started doing that gurgling thing. I thought I was going to vomit. I literally just turned and started running—I have no idea if I made it home for any of the aftermath but I definitely never wanted to play in that snowsuit ever again.

Needless to say I wasn't outside much that summer because of various reasons. My hair looked like I had a halo of light below and dark above. I'm not sure why my mom was actually all for me dying my hair but I can guess it was to prove to others that she cared about how I looked. So she paid to have my hair done. They just put some highlights around the top to let the color blend; I have auburn hair so it naturally changes colors based on my environment. I no longer looked like an embarrassment based on my hair. So she moved on to my physical body. If I hadn't already felt like a disgusting fat blob I definitely did when she was done with me. Just one more dig about my father's genetics. She would tell me, "You can't eat junk food, your father's family are big people, and you are already too heavy." Freshman year was going to start with me hating my body and thinking everyone was looking at me. But I had to just keep going. I wasn't going to let her bring me down.

Starting to Spiral

Stripping pieces of me

I have made it to my teen years but I left my childhood behind long ago. By summer of eighth grade I was spending every night Whitey didn't work either outside with him or in his apartment. Legally and ethically what he was doing to me was wrong, but I kept saying I wanted this. I thought I did—when he would touch my clit it felt good for a while and then there was pain. He told me this was normal after an orgasm. I believed him. But it is not what happens after I have an orgasm; mine are full-body and can go one after another once I'm in a good place. I didn't find that place until I was thirty-eight. I couldn't tell anyone what was happening with Whitey for so many reasons, but I did try quite a few times.

By the time I entered high school, I was well on the path to becoming one of those people with the family secrets. You know, the ones that make siblings, parents, aunts, and cousins all feel like they failed a person? For the most part, you didn't, but parents, you need to be present in your kids' lives even if they try to push you away. However, to extended family, for the most part I'm pretty sure there weren't big glowing signs and your loved one doesn't blame you. Second, even if there were signs and you tried to help (it's possible) your loved one couldn't take it at the time. Why do I say this? Because many of us that have grown up, were groomed, or indoctrinated into believing our worth and truth is based on what an intimate partner, parent, or superior says, can't even tell you what they are eating for lunch never mind what happened yesterday. If you have been through trauma and this is not the way you react, that is perfectly normal and fine too!

My body, your body, and everyone else's do what makes sense at the time. I try every day to block out my feelings of inadequacy. Even giving myself an outlet to write my feelings and have it heard by others, I still question why I matter. Honestly, who really wants to hear what I have to say? I think I'm not pretty enough, not smart enough, not interesting enough, not hurt enough, not saved enough. No matter what I tell myself all day or hear from my friends, I go back to that very first relationship when I was told I was too fat for anyone else. I was an ugly slut! He was also the first person I ever "willingly" had sex with.

When I was moved downstairs Whitey told me I was not allowed to go to the first floor and instead if I had to pee I was to go up to him or use a pot in the corner of my room. His reasoning being if I woke my mother up, she would ask questions. I didn't dare do anything else. I started going to school, coming straight home, and then staying in my room. I would only come out if I had to have family dinner. If he didn't see me as soon as he pulled in I had to explain why. If he agreed that I needed to be out of the area—taking a shower, talking to my mother, at my grandparents, or something for school—then I was okay. If he didn't agree, he'd grab my arm and search my body for bruises I'd gotten by being a klutz. This was done so he "wouldn't be the one bruising me." Once he found one he would hit and pick at the bruise or cut till I started to cry. If by chance he couldn't find one he would smack my face, thighs, breasts, belly, or ass since normally I didn't bruise there. This was all done so it wasn't him marking me, which prevented me from being able to tell anyone. However, just to be on the safe side he also stated that if I told anyone, I would be the one going to jail and being taken away, "because they are never going to believe your lies."

I learned quickly to just stand and take the punishments. I stared at walls and started seeing faces in them, or chanted in my head, "This does not hurt. I feel nothing. I am okay. Do not cry!" I did this because if I started to cry he'd tell me only babies cried...

In December 2018, I wrote the following about how Whitey formed the main influence on my personality and self-worth. What started as what I perceived as building me up in middle school very quickly turned to tearing me down for any and all imperfections to prove that I had no worth:

> *I grew up being told only babies cried. That if I wanted something to cry about he'd give me it. That my life wasn't worth anything but to please him. I can make any man cum it's just about learning his cues... but what does that give me at the end of the day? Insecurity and fear. I came to a scary realization today—I've probably known for years subconsciously. I crave to be in control of my life so much that I don't like alcohol or drugs, but I don't need to control pain. I know how that feels and the adrenaline rush of knowing pain is coming gives me the relief of not knowing what will come next. Being choked knowing that there is no feeling with it is just release. Being fucked as hard as humanly possible so he feels a release instead of gently and lovingly because really who will ever love me? And it just draws out the inevitable indescribable pain that comes from any man trying to make love to me.*

I was going into eighth grade and he was turning twenty-four. He controlled every thought I ever had in high school. So yes: I'm stating that this is consensual, because I thought it was at the time. But really he was sexually assaulting me and holding me mentally prisoner for years. He groomed me. My thoughts were not my own, my actions were only as Whitey said, and lying became so second nature that it has taken decades to start pulling the pieces apart and begin the healing process.

As the schoolyear started, he started putting in more and more restrictions. No going out after school unless it was to babysit or volunteer at the retirement home. Except, I wasn't allowed to babysit if he knew the father would be around even if it was just to relieve me from being there. I was required to page him as soon as I got home from school every day, which meant if I was late on the page he would punish me. One of his favorite punishments was to not allow me to see him that night and instead make me sleep in the hallway upstairs outside his apartment door. More often though he chose forcing me to fuck him then throwing me out to cry downstairs alone.

The whole thing makes my head spin. It feels like my writing is helping sometimes and others it's like I'm picking at that scab from when I got poison ivy and then fell off my bike, cutting it open over and over again. I write some and it's like I'm throwing all these jigsaw pieces all over the floor that I didn't even know existed. Helpful in the long run but for now it's not true order, just lots more questions. This means as I write I keep having to move the timeline around and adjust. You know, chunks here and there? But how do they fit to make them my whole story? Hopefully by the end I will be able to let go of the fear and shame I have carried around for far too long. Are you ready to jump in the rabbit hole of high school with me?

As ninth grade started I was super excited to be going in and making new friends, knowing I wouldn't have to relive middle school. I just didn't realize high school would test me even more and take away my independence completely. Even things I enjoyed and wanted to do were controlled by others. No clubs or afterschool activities other than babysitting and volunteering at the retirement home nearby because Whitey and my mother needed me at home. My mother because she was in pain and driving other kids, so I had to fit into her schedule. Whitey because if I wasn't home he couldn't be sure I was doing as I was told.

Sometime in eighth grade Whitey had me sleeping in his bed. Which meant by high school sleeping in my room was the exception. At the beginning it really was just me sleeping there alone, but slowly he added in new requirements. The first change he added in was I was no longer allowed to sleep in my pajamas. At bedtime he would have me strip in front of him. Then, he would run his hands down my body making sure it looked and felt exactly the same as the day before. During this time he would always point out the days I was bloated from either my period or my gastrointestinal issues. Actually pointing it out sounds a little like "I see you are bloated," etc...just an observation. That wasn't the case. He would take a butter knife in his hand while tracing and sometimes drawing circles around "the new fat." I was then required not to eat or take diuretics to get rid of the extra fat. He said it was because I was already unattractive. He was just trying to make sure I never got worse.

As time went on he started joining me in the bed. He would start with massaging my back. I liked that I felt safe and he was taking care of me, which I desperately needed. Then he would lie down fully clothed next to me and just hold me. The next addition was rolling me over and massaging my front. He decided that could only be done with him naked, or he would get lotion all over his clothes. He definitely wasn't going to let it stay that way as high school started. This was only the second stage of grooming which had me trusting him exclusively.

The proceeding was first written during April of 2021, during Sexual Assault Awareness Month. It was done mainly in a subconscious frame of mind, or dissociative state, during my daily posts to bring awareness to the sheer volume of sexual assaults in America. I fell into a story that I definitely was not ready to tell, or feel for that matter.

I've walked through the years of child sexual abuse knowing it hurt and changed my life but there were still some fun family parts—meeting Norm, getting to watch car races with my face pinned to the fence, wearing his welding shield to see a solar eclipse, getting a dog, and the dog having puppies. Those were things that happened outside of trauma and were amazing. As high school started the fun moments became fewer and farther in between.

I've processed that pain of being a child and not knowing what was going on. I forgave the child that very likely repeated actions that were taught to him. I wrote my story of my first assault, read it out loud dozens of times, and video recorded it. Each time I did one of those steps I reclaimed a piece of me. The original writing of "My First Rape Story" was written over three years ago; I still catch my breath hearing or reading it. Even with the lump in my throat while reading it I can see it as what it was: sexual assault caused by a child that very likely was sexually abused themselves. So yes I've forgiven Calvin for the part he played in changing my life, but it doesn't mean it never happened. It just means that I've processed it. But Whitey?

Why is it that writing about Whitey makes me want to curl up and die? He was an adult! He knew better! He took my innocence away! I married him! My parents let me? Really? I'm not sure I'll ever be ready to fully process it, but to be the best version of me I need to. I feel so strong after writing some days, and others feel like I just want to never remember again. Whitey didn't just do things because it's all he knew, he did it because he could. Talking and thinking about him causes me to relive every second of every day that far outweighs my worst nightmares. Honestly, I know I'm stronger than I was three years ago when I started writing, but still trying to process the lack of support and love in my life makes me want to run and hide. This means as I struggle with my day-to-day life and writing; I am now suddenly consciously aware that at fifteen I was beaten to cause a miscarriage—I want to vomit! Or just forget again!

As I started typing, and realizing what was coming out, I had to message the friends who are my editors. I told them I couldn't talk, but I needed them. I just needed to know I wasn't alone. Thankfully Google Docs are mainly stored in...the ether? Whoa! Wait a minute, what happened? This means that if I want to write something with someone they can be in the same document while I am and they can edit. For me at that moment I just needed them there. So while I wrote, no longer alone, they quietly checked grammar and wrapped it up so I could share that day, without making me read what I had written. I wasn't ready to read it. My friends assured me it wasn't necessary for me to read it yet and specifically reminded me I had counseling on Friday and should wait until then to read the story. I'm sure others can relate to this.

Reclaiming Me

Trauma changes your brain and certain triggers are just too much for one person to handle alone. As the days, weeks, months, and years go by from the time I first started sharing I've learned it's not easy to leave myself so open and vulnerable, but for me it is necessary for me to share. This is not only to heal myself but to help those that can't make their voice heard. They need to know they are not alone. Everyone deserves to be loved and respected as they are. We all deserve love.

You might ask how? How do I keep going, while picking at old wounds that would be much easier left scabbed over and ignored? Well, I realized that I can't truly heal until I know what happened and break it down outside of my head. So I use certain techniques to help me write and make the processing easier. The first thing I do is never write when I have other responsibilities to worry about. I've tried writing with my kids around, but it doesn't work for me. The littles are constantly interrupting my writing process. They could be laughing and happy, or hysterically crying. It doesn't matter, it still stops the flow and I don't know how to get it back. Then we have my teens: they know how to leave me alone when I'm writing, but they still really want attention and believe dinner two hours from now, practicing driving, or sending me a TikTok of a bunny is important to view immediately.

Even though my teens may cause interruptions, the main reason I don't like writing around them is that it makes me sad and stuck. I've tried to protect them the best I can. Until my oldest turned thirteen I thought I had for the most part. However, something still happened to them because the health system we are told to trust cares more about money than actually helping people (That's for another book). For the most part I'm thankful I've been able to watch over and protect them, but I also can see how easily they could get hurt. Adding in my thoughts of what if something happens to them. And yeah, writing with them around brings out the Mama Bear so whoever hurts them should probably watch their back. I may not be able to stand up for myself, but do not threaten my loved ones!

How do I usually try to write? Well, I tend to find a clean and peaceful environment but last night I found out that a loud bar sitting at a table by myself is just as conducive to writing as a quiet space, and possibly even better at distracting my brain allowing for free thoughts. If I'm alone, headphones in and my phone on night mode are very important. First, music allows the noise in my head to dull out so I can just write. It also keeps my ADHD from triggering for the most part; if I get a call or text there is no telling when I will remember what I was focusing on writing. I tend to have a constant supply of gum or hard candy, which just allows me to chew absently. There are academic journals that say gum is proven to help you focus. I also wear clothes that I find comforting with thumbholes or keep my blanket/stuffed bunny nearby to hold when I'm trying to come up with the right flow of words. The clothing and blankie are examples of grounding items I use.

When I am lucky enough to be spending time with someone I trust, I will make a comfy place on the floor in front of them or at least be nearby so I can feel their warmth. I think my favorite setting is sitting on the floor in front of a partner just typing away. If I get stressed or just need a break I can look up or feel their hands and the warmth of their body on mine. No talking, just warmth and strength.

The most important piece to my writing method is that I don't attempt to read my writing till it's all done and I feel strong enough. In certain months, like April, I tend to just get the article done and wait to read till April is over. NO! Sharing my story isn't easy but it's needed!

I feel like I just walked in a huge circle because I still really just can't sort it out in my head. High school is seriously like a black hole for me; the only way to truly tell my story is to fully immerse myself in it. I let my subconscious/dissociative state take over.

Magical simmering pot, candles, and meditation music going sets me in the right headspace today. Since Whitey took his time with my "education" to lay out all the groundwork needed to control my life for ten years. It makes sense that it would take time to see the truth. It also isn't surprising that my memories seem almost like they are the scenes cut from the final edit.

It Can't Get Worse Until It Does

High school (or my personal hell)

High school is meant to be the time when kids make mistakes, when they figure out who they are, and when the world around them influences the way they feel about themselves. Social media and Covid have made today's teens very different from when I was entering high school. I started high school in the fall of 1994. I turned fifteen within days of starting school. Which at the time pretty much meant I was the oldest kid in class because the cutoff for starting kindergarten was five by December 31. Remember how I said I was really stubborn? Well, when you decide not to take the placement test in kindergarten because the teacher didn't explain it thoroughly, you get kept back. Ooops?

Okay, here we go for real, starting high school. I was so excited I didn't stand out! We were all new to the school; yes, a few came from the same schools but not that many. We all looked similar in our button-down shirts and pants or plaid skirts. My first year had a strict dress code but not a full uniform, other than the sweater that was worn from October till May. I knew the layout of the school because I had to do work-study to pay for some of the scholarships I had received. I also had been able to mainly get used books because part of my job was to sort all the books that were returned at the end of the year. This slight advantage made it so much easier for me to feel safe in the new environment. I have social anxiety, was diagnosed with ADHD as an adult, and am quite possibly on the

Reclaiming Me

autism spectrum if we go through the rest of my quirks; but school classrooms, I'm good. I'm smart, just awkward as fuck....

I quickly made friends with the others in all honors classes. We were all a little weird and kids liked that I knew where classes were. Our class was the biggest freshman class ever, not crazy bigger than the one before but enough that there weren't enough lockers on the freshman floor, so we also shared lockers for the most part. I remember my locker mate well. We decided to do a top and bottom portion, with of course our coats and bags both hanging in the middle. She had the top and I had the bottom. She was adorable and always wore her skirt. I very nicely chose not to tell her that every time she reached up when I was kneeling to get books I could pretty much read the brand of underwear she was wearing. Not that I was looking, just there.

The school building was my sanctuary. Due to my mother's new job of driving kids around I was always dropped off super early, but that was okay because some of my friends had to take public transportation so we would all hang out in the school cafeteria having breakfast and doing classwork or just chatting. It was the one point in my day that was purely about fun and being a teen. As a reminder, I grew up before cell phones and the world wide web. When we hung out with friends we chatted, we read books, we played hangman, and we helped each other with homework. If something didn't seem right we'd ask our friends and they would give us the best answer they had. This meant things like a twenty-five-year-old having sex with a fifteen-year-old in my friends group wasn't discussed...

I had believed Whitey when he said that the age of statutory rape in Massachusetts was fifteen. It wasn't, it was sixteen. Not that it would have mattered unless I told my friends or teachers about it because "he loved me and I would do anything to protect him." Over the next four years, I would not only continue to have sex with a man ten years older than me, I would also become the school's sex expert and condom supplier. I'll explain more about both of those in a bit.

School was the one place I felt perfectly safe even though I didn't agree with their religious teachings. Actually, one of my favorite classes freshman year was religious studies. I loved learning about the rules of Catholicism and the teacher was a sweet older woman who was married to another religious teacher that I would have senior year. When I say sweet I mean she treated us with respect as long as we did the same. We knew the rules. You were to be seated and ready to learn the second the bell rang. If not you would be sent to the office with a detention slip or to get a late pass…which would translate into detention usually. She taught us the basic principles of Catholicism. Many students in the class hated it because they were doing very similar things in CCD, and figured they already knew it all. I on the other hand made her light up because I would bounce some of my knowledge of being a Methodist and also some little things I'd learned from years of hanging out with a group of Jewish students, my cousin taught to her for comparison.

As a default I always loved any math courses. If the circumstances were different I probably would have been on the math team and have gone on to do advanced placement in math or college courses while in high school. They weren't different though, and just getting through the school days and not having too many points knocked off for failing to pass in homework was why my grade sat where it did. It was always an A- or B+, just not enough for the special extras. The math teachers were the ones that would use my tests to grade the other kids' tests. One time was quite hysterical actually. I had transposed a number and shown all my work from that number through the whole problem. The answer I gave was correct for the numbers I used so the teacher assumed I had the correct answer. But as he graded the other kids' papers after mine he kept seeing them all wrong with the same answer.

Finally he took my paper and read it through next to the test. All of a sudden the light bulb went off: I had changed one number. The next day he was laughing when he handed them back but you could tell he felt a little stupid.

Yes, I loved math but that was not my favorite class freshman year, instead it was English. The teacher was really young, possibly younger than Whitey, but no matter what right in that range. He must have realized I was insecure because every time he saw me he'd tell me to keep my chin up and everything would be okay. All the girls in my class and probably school had a crush on him. He knew he was the talk of the kids but that year he just focused on teaching. I believe he left for two years and came back when I was a senior. Whatever the case he loved books and allowed us to read any book we wanted as long as it fit his parameters. I loved this since I could only read Of Mice and Men, or Fahrenheit 451 so many times.

I needed to learn. I needed the escape. Because when I went home I was alone...which meant the time at school I cherished.

Once home I would get my food together and do homework then wait. My stepfather and I would say our prayers around eight thirty and then he would go up and watch TV with my mother for another hour or so. They would both be out cold most nights by half past nine. I was then to wait another thirty minutes or so to make sure they really were asleep. Then go out the bulkhead of the basement. Go back in the house through the backdoor that Whitey had left unlocked for me. Quietly, walk up the first flight of stairs just in case my mother had woken up and wanted to chat with Whitey. Then once I hit the second floor landing I could just run up the stairs to his apartment.

There was always one of three distinct smells wafting from his apartment. The first was a clean, almost sterile smell, the one of Dial soap and bleach. He didn't like it to ever smell like fire or other smells that one encounters as a firefighter or paramedic.

That smell was the one most often present; he was OCD about cleanliness.

The next smell was one that still haunts my dreams: the smell of Captain and Diet Coke. His drink of choice, when I was a freshman in high school, I loved the smell. It made me feel like part of him, especially on the nights he would give me one small sip. I hated the taste but I loved him. It wasn't till years later that I realized he was also an alcoholic and carried his alcohol in his work bag, drinking during his shifts. Which also meant if he had a bad day at work he came home after drinking more and therefore I paid for his bad day.

The third smell was his "red sauce," or "gravy." Once a week he would spend twenty-four hours making the sauce so the entire apartment and stairwells would smell of an Italian kitchen. The garlic, tomato, peppers, onion, olive oil, and a few other ingredients I didn't quite pick up on made my stomach growl because I was usually hungry going upstairs. He had me on a diet because I was fat. So I was never actually offered it, which was okay with me. I loved the smell; however, I never actually wanted any since I didn't eat sauce on my pasta. Whenever my dislike of sauce was brought up it was usually preceded with a bowl full of pasta and sauce to be whipped by my head.

I loved sleeping upstairs, it meant I didn't have to be in my new bedroom in the basement, and by this time my mom had made another questionable decision and had a convict living in the other bedroom downstairs. Yes, I just said that there was an adult male that had spent five years in prison in the bedroom next to a fifteen-year-old. He had been convicted of check fraud. Luckily, he was nice and was one of the only adults that didn't take advantage of me, but definitely not a choice I would make for my children.

One night, not long after I turned fifteen, Whitey decided I needed to do something for him, or at least that's what he said. I knew not to question him so I said finally, "Okay, yes Sir, I will do whatever you want Sir." He told me I needed to have sex with him since I loved him and he couldn't date anyone because I took up all his time. My answer was, "Yes of course. I love you."

That night he stood me up facing the TV, with my back to the couch and the dining area. He slowly removed my pants, then slid the shirt over my head. I felt safe and loved. I felt this was where I was supposed to be. He rubbed his fingers over my nipples telling me how I had the perfect breasts. Then unclasped my bra in one easy motion. I got a little insecure because he was staring at me. He looked at my face suddenly and held it in his hands. He told me I was beautiful and he would never let anyone hurt me again.

Then Whitey led me into the bedroom. He massaged my back while repeating that he would keep me safe. As he told me no one would hurt me again he entered me. It didn't feel good but I didn't know better. I had already learned it was supposed to hurt. That night I stared at the pillow under me memorizing the stripes... crisp, clean, blue, and cream stripes. Do not cry! This does not hurt! You are in the water, there is a slight breeze on the lake. You can feel the cool air on your face. The wetness on your legs is just lake water. Keep breathing!

When he finished he got one of the hospital towels and wiped himself up. Then threw it at me telling me to hold it between my legs and make sure I didn't get blood on the bed. That night he didn't want to lie next to me in bed so I followed him back out to the living room. He looked at me and said shouldn't you be sleeping. I looked back and asked to be held. "Okay, but you are not watching the TV." I was okay with that. I asked to use the bathroom to clean up first. His answer was the same as always: make sure you use the strawberry shampoo I bought for you since it's what you have downstairs.

"Yes, Sir." As I walk into the bathroom to wash my hands first...I loved the smell of his soap; yellow Dial antibacterial. It always made me smile and think of him when I wasn't with him. But he said I couldn't smell like that when I left the apartment. I grab my towel and use the strawberry shampoo to wash my entire body. Then do the conditioner. As time went on, he stocked up on every shampoo, face wash, acne solution, deodorant I ever used so that way when I left his apartment I smelled the same as I had when I went up to it. There were times he bought two so I could change the one in the shower downstairs.

When I finished my shower I lay down with my head on his lap but facing him instead of the TV. I felt safe and warm. He rubbed my head and just let me drift. I remember him kissing the top of my head gently and saying, "I love you" as I fell asleep. The sound of The Red Green Show, in the background. He smelled of Old Spice, Dial, Head & Shoulders, Captain Morgan's & Diet Coke, and his red sauce. That night he woke me around one or two to send me downstairs since he was going to bed and didn't want to have to get up again. I sleepily walked down the stairs, went outside, and snuck back into my bedroom through the bulkhead.

This is how the first half of my freshman year went. Every night I was with him; however, he felt it was necessary. After that night he would send me to the bedroom and follow to give me a massage. I quickly learned that was code for leading to sexual intercourse. He tended to flip me over to rub my front right before penetrating me. I learned every crack and crevice of the ceiling as if it was the only thing keeping me alive. I forgot what was happening, and just reminded myself that this is what love felt like. I felt like a puppet, no less than a puppet! At least as a puppet you wouldn't feel pain.

Then in the morning I'd get up and go to school like every other high school freshman. I didn't talk about what happened at night. I worked on school reports in the school cafeteria while waiting for my mother to pick me up. She had started a new business, one that Whitey worked part time for; it was a taxi type service for kids. Parents were working out of the house and couldn't pick up kids from school and get them to daycare, or karate, or singing lessons, so she did it. Shuttling kids from place to place, including getting me additional babysitting jobs where, once she had the younger child and I in the van, she would drive us to the child's house where I would stay until the parents got home; and then would wait to be picked up again.

I went to the homecoming game that year and slept over at a friend's house after. We had so much fun! She lived close enough to the fields that we got ready at her house, getting all sparkly and writing "Let's Go Shamrocks" on our faces in green and drawing a couple shamrocks on too. We hung out all the time until the boy she liked flirted with me. She was a cheerleader. He was a football player. I was the weirdo that knew far too much about sex. I'm pretty sure he just figured I was easy, but I never found out because there was no way I would go anywhere near a guy I knew a friend liked, especially since I was happily in dreamland with Whitey or so I thought.

In March, I really wanted to be something other than a dirty secret, so I asked to be able to tell my parents. He dropped me as soon as I got upset. He told me no one would believe me and I would lose him forever if I told my parents. Then to prove that I couldn't live without him he stopped opening the door at night. He also made a point to leave for work early and come home late so we didn't cross paths in the hallways most days. I was devastated. I thought I had "lost the only person that truly loved me." Finally, I sat on the floor upstairs and cried, begging him to take me back. I remember him coming out that night and telling me he had a date and to go away. I was hurt and mad.

I wrote this on March 30, at the age of fifteen:

He thinks he can just waltz in anytime he feels like it and I'll jump.

I see him walking down the hall, my heart starts beating a mile a min_
like a cotton ball. I can't help but look as he stops, and I can't seem
But how much I'd like to tell him "I love you." The only problem is my hear_
and I can't help but wonder will he help or just hurt _

His smile makes my he_
His body mak_
have him till

The fear etched in my heart. Never to let go until I know for cert_
to destroy a person's life. I only wish that day would come when _
When I will not have to hide any of my feelings instead I can run

Love is it Always th_
Does it have limits? Is it _
Is it all inclusive? D_
No Love is a fe_

Is he really that insensitive to destro_
just to find he could care less? _
all he did was pretend it never happ_
She doesn't know if she can ever face h_
She'd only be hu_

My mouth dries up
ink of anything
en broken into tiny pieces,
re?

mp into my throat. His face makes me want to take it and kiss it and never let it g
whole body scream for joy. Then I come to the realization that I can never
eart repairs itself from the many hurts that my young life has gone through.
I think if only I could go back to before and live life to its fullest.

ot all guys are cruel enough
eart will be as free as a bird.
telling of my feelings for him.

Does it leave when times are hard? Is it Everlasting?
ul? Does it cause sorrow? Is it caring? Does it bring hurt?
belong to the strong? the rich? the poor? or the weak?
that can be shared; By everyone; and will not Die!

heart, even after she laid it on the line
dn't even bother to acknowledge her,
t. That she never tried to know him
If he doesn't love her why should she?
gain. Right?

Athena Tempest Rose

> *Well the jumping isn't happening anymore,*
> *'cause my love isn't a bottomless pit that never ends.*
> *It is a give and take situation.*
> *I give, he takes, that's not how love works either.*

I've always been intrigued reading my journals and trying to remember exactly where they came from. The journal the above entry came from spans just over a year of my life, specifically one of the most defining years in my life. It makes me hurt in ways I didn't know were possible. However, then I remember where I am compared to where I came from and I can't help but let out a huge smile and realize how strong I always have been.

The writings didn't start back up until May 9 of that same year; those are more in my "I need him" style. I had gotten him back by agreeing that this was supposed to be a secret. I loved him, so I wouldn't want to hurt him. I had given up caring if I was a secret. I just needed to see him. He also said on my eighteenth birthday we'd tell my parents together. So I just wrote about my thoughts and what we did. Even if my mom found my journal there were no names and she just thought I was a liar anyway.

I wrote the following selections that May. Remember that Whitey didn't enter my life until I was already alone. I had been abandoned by my parents, my grandparents knew nothing that was going on, and my teachers? I thought they saw me as white trash from Rhode Island. I thought I wasn't worth anything to them. I know one teacher I had as an eighth grader that might read this. If she does she will surely say, "That is not true, Athena!"

I keep trying to make sense of my thoughts and why I would allow myself in that situation. I can't because it's not my fault. I was a child trying to learn how the world worked. I loved him... part of me still to this day can't see him as just a monster. We loved each other didn't we? I mean I married him just over five years after these journal entrieswere written.

As freshman year wound down I became focused on getting my permit and getting excited for camp. I was only going to be attending one week as a camper that year. It was Living Arts, the same one my children now attend. However, I was going to be there for at least two other weeks as a counselor. My brother and my dad had moved back to the area by the end of the school year. Actually, something I found out last summer: my brother had moved back over a year prior and had been living at his friend's house. But my dad was back! Which meant I got to have quiet time at his house when I didn't want to go home yet. My brother was also in charge of getting me from school some days, because I got out later than his high school.

One such day of my brother driving me sticks clearly in my head as I'm sure it does his and the friends that it involves. You can believe me or not, but I believe without a doubt that I knew something was going to happen and was able to protect my brother because of that knowledge. My dad wasn't living in the school district that my brother's friends lived in, but I was. It was a Wednesday when he had to bring me home on the way to pick up his friends to go hang out. He drove me home the way he always did but today was different; I felt like my insides were being ripped out at one point in the drive. I knew there was going to be a car accident that day and believed my brother and everyone in the car wouldn't be able to just walk away.

So, great. I have this premonition or whatever you want to call it, but what sixteen-year-old is going to listen to his fifteen-year-old sister? That's what I had to figure out before getting out of his car. I thought about it and finally as we pulled into my driveway...

"Phil, can you promise me that everyone that gets in your car today wears their seatbelt?"

His response: "Yeah, whatever."

"No really!!! I'm not getting out of the car till you promise!" I responded, knowing I needed to make an impact.

"Fine! Okay? Can you get out now?"

"Yup!" And I happily went inside to work on my schoolwork or something.

It was a Wednesday and I usually spent those evenings alone and watched Beverly Hills 90210 religiously like so many other kids my age. A few minutes before eight that night I turned the TV on and picked up the phone. It hadn't rung yet but he was on the other end of the call. "Phil, what happened? Are you all okay?"

"The car is totaled."

"I know but everyone is okay right?"

"Yes, we need someone to get us."

"I know. You are near the trash dump right?"

"Yes? How did you know? Never mind, just please get someone here."

When we got there all the kids came over and gave me hugs. Then the policeman came over to talk to us and said, "I've never been to one of these accidents where everyone walked away. You guys are very lucky you had your seatbelts on. They definitely saved your lives." My brother and I have a special bond that through any distance and life changes he gets me and I get him.

Freshman year coming to a close meant freshman/sophomore social. I was excited to be able to go and asked my camp best friend to go with me. He graciously said yes, but then had an overseas field trip with his high school. He was one of the many that came home with severe food poisoning. Which meant he felt like crap and by that Friday night he was tired and had no desire to go dancing. We ended up getting bread, butter, fruit, and shrimp cocktail and just hanging out at my dad's watching movies. Yes I was kinda sad to miss the dance, but had so much fun just chatting and hanging out.

With the dance behind us, we all know what happens next! It's summer break! This summer was all about camp and babysitting. I'm not even sure I remember being home to be controlled by

Whitey; he had distanced himself and must have been watching mainly on the outside looking in. I loved being a camp counselor even more than I liked being at camp as a camper. My first year of counseling was definitely an interesting one.

I remember one week more vividly than any other. It was a new style in which older elementary school students were supposed to be living in nature. They were learning to build fires and how to cook food on them. We were also supposed to be making our own teepees or other structures. This meant we didn't have the typical camp beds, walls, bathrooms/outhouses, or set meals. The campers and the adult counselors were aware of the situation and had been told to bring cots or air mattresses if they were wanted. I was not told the same so I just packed for camp. Ugh! This wasn't horrible until night two or three when it started raining. The kids hadn't even been shown beginner teepee making or fire building. I was running around trying to keep the fire going and help make some sort of structure so we could keep our clothes and bedding dry. The two adults were in their tent all cozy while I sat outside. Finally we were able to figure out a way to hold the tarp up to create a partially dry area for kids to sleep. We had twelve kids, myself, and two adult counselors. I worked with the kids to push as much of their stuff as possible towards the middle to stay dry. There was only a limited amount of room and we also needed a place to sleep so the bags were placed towards the side, with mine on the edge protecting most of the kids' stuff.

Why was I as a teen the one coming up with solutions that the adults should have? I don't know, but when the next thought was to let the kids sleep in the shelter and the two adults sleep in the tent, I recall being told I could go in the tent, to which I responded no thank you. The next thing that was said was, "Okay, find a comfortable place to sleep and let the kids stay wherever." "Ummm...we can't let fifth graders sleep coed." I was looked at like I was crazy, but insisted anyway. I prepped my sleeping bag to be in the middle, then directed the boys to one side and girls to the other. I loved knowing I may have made a difference in the kids' lives and was sad when it was time to leave camp.

During July and August I continued my journals. I was writing about how Whitey was never around and I had to hurt around his schedule. He kept telling my mother I was just an infatuated child. Which in turn meant my mother wouldn't let me talk to him. Really? I was just a child? Why keep sleeping with me and telling me all about how we would be happy and our kids would be so smart and amazing? Why keep repeating that my mom would kill you? Whenever there was a question of someone finding out about our relationship, he would always say it was my fault. I literally thought I destroyed his life for years.

During this time period I was so confused. After the first time I had sex with Whitey I started remembering what happened when I was younger more clearly. I started dreaming more and having recurring prophetic nightmares, which meant I ran to Whitey even more as he continued to push and pull. I was so confused trying to figure out the difference between what was real and what wasn't. Even at the age of fifteen I didn't remember exactly what happened when I was being assaulted in the old house. I knew it had happened; I was beyond afraid, and trying to figure out everything on my own.

Whitey pretty much ignored me the entire month of July. While I was tossing and turning every night, he was going out with someone and would leave me crying on his doorstep when I went up to understand what I had done wrong. During the month, I had been filling in pieces of what happened in the city. One of my journal entries from that time period talks about how beds made me feel, and even more specifically, mine. I didn't get a new bed in the move, so it was always the bed I was raped on and ignored until I turned eighteen.

Reclaiming Me

Writing from July 25, 1995, I was 15:

I toss and turn on night
Never to forget the fear
As the bed squeaks it gets worse
I start seeing it like it was yesterday
He tries to help but doesn't know what I need
I need to be held and told it will never happen again
I don't need to be told it's not my fault
I know that I just want to know why?
Why do I have to deal with the pain?
When all he felt was release and joy.
And more importantly why didn't she hear my screams of fear?

I was remembering bits and pieces of what happened while I was in elementary school. I wrote about how Calvin would never look back and see how he destroyed me. He destroyed my hopes and dreams of happiness, because I would never forget what happened but I also couldn't remember all the details. I didn't think I would ever be able to feel true love because I was so very broken. I wrote about never forgetting—his face, his hands, or his long legs pinning me down. At this time I was even more distraught and triggered because Fresh Prince of Bel-Air was on TV and every time I saw the actor, I saw Calvin. The neighborhood always made a joke about how much Calvin looked like him. For me that ended up meaning I couldn't watch shows or movies with Will Smith in them (I have since been able to watch a few movies, most notably the live-action Aladdin, without having a full dissociative event).

Almost everything I did caused fear. I didn't have anyone to go to but Whitey. I trusted him for some unknown reason. I shouldn't say "unknown reason." He was what I thought was my savior. I wrote about how he cared so much for everybody else and never thought of himself. He started breaking down. I thought it was because of how much he loved me. I thought that he was the one good thing in my life. I also thought that he was going to leave me, because I would never be enough.

The summer leading into my sophomore year of high school was nothing special other than camp. When I was at camp, Whitey did whatever it was he did when I wasn't around. However, when I was home and he was not working we were together. If I was babysitting the kids on the second floor he would come down and we would have all the doors open. allowing everyone to come and go on that floor. I wasn't really allowed to hang out with kids my age. He'd remind me of what Calvin did to me and say all boys this age do that. I was also hardcore working out and dieting—I planned on going into the military out of high school and then getting my psychology degree.

Whitey made me run stairs every day he was home so that way he was sure to see me. When I say run stairs I mean starting from the basement floor, running up the outer stairs where the bulkhead was, up the stairs to the back door and up to the third floor, back down the third floor, through the hall of the second, down the front, up the side, down the basement, and repeat. I have always had hypermobile joints but was never diagnosed. For me this meant some days I was physically running on a broken ankle. It also meant my knees and hips would pop while running and I'd have to use the railings to keep myself from falling. I learned that no matter what was wrong I could keep going.

If I stopped there was no one to pick me back up. If I complained of pain my mom would say, well I guess you're never going

Reclaiming Me

to make it in the army. Not really nice, but Whitey's remarks were more stingy. He said that I was worthless, that if I couldn't even do these drills they were going to take one look at me and send me on my way. I was simply not good enough for the military. My dad was the only one truly trying to help, in the way he thought was best. He had me join Jenny Craig with him.

It was only about a week into sophomore year that I got my license. For the first six months or so driving at night was limited, as was driving other kids. However, I recall an incident that either happened right before summer ended or during September. My mom and Norm had a party. It was mainly drinking, music, and a bonfire. It went to the wee hours of morning. I was in bed sleeping when all of a sudden I got woken up by my mother or stepfather running in my room screaming at me. To say I was confused would be an understatement. All I made out of the screaming at that point was I needed to drive someone to the hospital, because all the adults were too drunk to drive. I'm still super confused and asked why. Then reminded them that I wasn't allowed to drive this late.

They said it didn't matter because I was the only one that could drive.

Apparently, my stepdad's best friend, Harry, had decided he could walk through fire. Clearly he could not walk through fire and had fallen in. Luckily, it seemed he only burnt his hands. They looked horrible and he was screaming, which I'm sure would have been a hundred times worse if he was sober. When we got to the hospital they brought him back and I just got to sit and wait. The ER was able to clean it all up and then they sent him home with pain meds and his hands completely wrapped with antibiotic stuff. When we get home my mom decides that of course he can't drive home, especially on pain meds, and he's still drunk. He was given the area in the basement with the futon between myself and the ex-convict. Does anyone else see where this is about to go? Seriously, she's letting two adult males sleep in the same area as her almost-sixteen-year-old daughter? I got divorced from my big kids' dad because he was a pass-out drunk and I wouldn't let babysitters be put in that situation. I don't want to risk that in any way shape or form.

So yes, he was going to spend the night on the futon outside my room. We got him all set on the futon. I went to lie down in bed, but just as I did he called me back. He asked me to get him water, so he'd have it when the meds were due. Fine, I go upstairs and get a glass of water. I go to put it on the side table and the next thing I remember is his hands sliding up my stomach under my pajama shirt. He started touching me as much as possible but very lightly, and he wasn't feeling much since, well, gauze for starters. When I didn't run away he pulled me into him. His kiss tasted of alcohol, cigarette smoke, burned skin, and something sweet. It felt like he was sucking part of me in with him. I couldn't get enough. I wanted to feel the warmth of his body, so when he ended up pushing further I was already there and waiting. His hands weren't very helpful so he used his teeth to expose my breasts so he could suck on them. It felt like a heat between us, I wanted everything he did. Mostly everything was done with his mouth and there was no direct touching below the belt. Then, I went to sleep like nothing happened.

The next day, they were all hungover and just hanging out. During this hanging out my stepfather hired him. On Monday he started working. When I got home from school he was outside, so I decided to go walk around the back of the barn. He went in the same direction and caught my face in his hands and pulled me into him for a kiss. For the next few weeks, or months, we would meet up and just make out. (I have a really hard time remembering timing and sequences because of the trauma.) It was fun and not demanding like things were with Whitey. Except, I was just turning sixteen and this was not appropriate at all. But this was my life, and every male that came into it, besides a father figure, was sexual towards me. You may think I'm exaggerating—I wish!

As I was enjoying another taboo relationship, Whitey started telling me that no one else would ever like me. I was too broken for someone else. My panic attacks while we were having sex were ridiculous and I needed to just get over it already. With these words he would push sex even more. It was all about his enjoyment. He would start a massage, but then within two minutes, he would turn it into shoving his penis in my vagina. I got to the point where I was dissociating pretty much the second he started giving me a massage because my body knew pain was coming next. He kept telling me to date people but the second I would he would rip me apart. The day after a date I was always called a slut and a whore, it didn't matter whether I was having sex or not. If I ever went on a second or third date I was locked out of his apartment for a week, or until he decided, I'd "given my penance."

At the end of September, while he was pushing and pulling me in different directions, my writings started back up again. I wrote I'm afraid that I ruined his life because I got pregnant. I blamed myself even though he was the one that was using a withdrawal method and hadn't sent me to get birth control pills yet. My mother heard something and grabbed the two of us in the hallway. To this day I'm not exactly sure what she saw, heard, or was told, but I remember vividly that he stood staring at her without a single glance at me and said, "I would never touch her. She's just a child with an infatuation." He walked away and I was grounded for telling lies.

One of my writings dated September 30, right after my sixteenth birthday:

His life changed forever because of a night of passion
Will he give up everything to show that he truly cares?
Or will he make her take on this awful task alone?
If he leaves her it will just show he never really cared.

But if he stays he will be giving up all his dreams
His only hope is that it is all a big mistake
So he doesn't have to make this awful choice
But if it isn't what will he do?

I'm not sure exactly whether I told him that throwing me across the room caused a miscarriage or just that I must have been wrong and was never pregnant to begin with. But I know that my mother thought I had lied the entire time and his career was never threatened.

During this time is also when I finally tried to share what happened at nine with my parents...but not necessarily in a healthy way. I didn't really start sharing till about thirty years after that very first assault, because like so many others that first person didn't believe me. I tried to tell a friend right away, but that friend told me it couldn't be true. She was nine (to eleven), just like me, so her experiences hopefully were nonexistent. That short conversation in the church bathroom one afternoon stopped me from talking then and I didn't repeat it for about five more years.

In early fall that year, I got into a yelling match with my mother and stepfather, which turned into them telling me I didn't understand pain. Remember this was after I had had a "spontaneous" abortion/miscarriage; I was angry and hurting. I didn't care who I hurt at that moment so out of my mouth came, "Calvin raped me for years." My mother responded with something along the lines of, "You just want attention." I wanted to scream at her! "You've never believed me! Even when Whitey lied to your face about me just being an infatuated child, and I tried to tell you I was pregnant. But no, you believed him!" That scream didn't come. Nothing came out, it was the first time I recall screaming in my head but unable to make the words come out. I've learned through the years that I become mute when I trigger. So the two of them got out of the van and enjoyed the pig roast at their friend's house, while I sat in the van and cried. I couldn't speak up again till decades later.

My mother couldn't wait till I was able to drive other kids to and from school. It meant she no longer had to pick up kids at the high school and could focus on other kids. I don't know how I ended up driving the five kids I drove because I didn't know all of them. Maybe she was making some money from them? Or maybe people I did know were just jumping on the Athena-can-drive train. I know my mom said I had to do certain things because she was paying for my insurance. I was the one paying for my gas from babysitting money. I also wanted to help in the household because my mom was always saying we were struggling with money.

By the end of September I was convinced I was ruining Whitey's life. In my journal I was asking myself whether it was fair for me to hurt somebody else. Whitey was falling apart and I believed it was my fault. That I needed to save him. Yup, I believed it was all my fault because that's how it worked in my house. No matter who caused a problem it was always, "ATHENA! Get in here now!" I believed that no one else would ever care about me.

I thought we had so much in common. He knew every single thought I ever had even before I had them. To me it looked like he cared exclusively about my well-being. In actuality, he was doing everything in his power to change my feelings and thoughts of what mattered. I couldn't possibly cut him out of my life because I truly believed he had saved me. Well, other than the few times when I was by myself; then things seemed less black and white and more hazy trying to figure out right from wrong.

I wrote this in September 1995:

The beauty of night has her spellbound
It shows itself to no one in particular
Yet its brilliance is to each a different feeling

One of love, fear, joy, anger, happiness, and pain
Never to let its mysteries go to any one person
Only to let each one feel what they desire.
She knows it scares her and saves her all at the same time
But how can she feel hurt on the darkest night?
When it's her saving grace on all others?
Its quiet wraps around her to let her heal
Its darkness let her sink into the void
Its cold brings everything back with a vengeance
She fears the unknown thought
Yet escapes into the unknown beyond
to heal her broken heart

Over the holiday season I let him go because he said that I had to. I spiraled during that time. I started going to the library or bookstore and sticking myself in the adult help sections reading everything I could related to sex and intimacy. I thought he was throwing me away and I didn't understand why he thought I was so worthless. I wanted the pain to end, but I still saw that crazy light that to me meant there was something to stay for. That light I saw/see has always kept me from trying to "unalive" myself. I would sit in my shower holding a kitchen knife but even though Whitey had showed me the "correct way" to kill myself I couldn't put it to my skin.

Everything about not seeing him made me cry. I felt like the world was going to end. I missed his touch. His love. His security. How could they take away the one thing that mattered? But he just sits there and agrees with them. How can they say all I care about is myself? I've always put others' feelings before mine. Why can't I just once think about healing myself? He was helping to free me from my fears. How did I let them build up inside me for so long? I didn't have anyone to give my soul to. How could I possibly think he deserved my trust? He didn't expect me to tell him anything, at least that's what I thought. Why can't I have the one thing that matters to me?

I believed that everything Whitey ever did was to help me. That the distance that was being put between us was there because I was causing problems. As the school year continued he had started sneaking around with me again. Not until after I spiraled and begged him to see me again. The past few months had me feeling more alone than I had ever felt before. So it definitely got far worse before it started getting better later in December:

How do you remember something hidden so deep in your soul?
What do you do when you finally do remember the awful truth?
When you can no longer run from the very thing that's been haunting you?
If you forgot it for a reason why would you want to remember?
Why do you want to put yourself through that pain again?
Would it help to remember and finally let you go on living?

After the holidays, I had gotten mad at Whitey again because he basically disappeared when I needed him most. My perception was that I gave up everything to save him. Then in turn he destroyed my heart. I protected him from reality. But he chose to respond by turning away from me. I tried to understand his feelings. He decided that my feelings were invalid. I trusted him with my heart and soul. He took them and gave nothing back. I couldn't do anything but block him out. He was saying one thing but doing another. I was getting hurt again because I loved him and couldn't see he was controlling my thoughts. I thought his intentions were good but he still didn't see me. I had already lost one of my best friends. He just didn't want to understand I needed someone to lean on. I didn't want anything but a friend. He didn't want just that, because being in control of me made him feel powerful. He definitely had a Napoleon Complex. I thought he was always there when I needed him; well, other than if other adults were around. I just couldn't lose anyone else. And couldn't deal with everything alone anymore.

In April of my sophomore year we went to Disney as a family. My mom, Norm, and I drove down, stopping for a night to see his relatives in another part of Florida. Then we headed over to Disney. I remember the three of us having such a fun drive down. However, I tend to forget the tears, which I'm 99 percent sure were there, especially since it was a two-day drive and the three of us slept in the same hotel room.

I got to drive through an amazing tunnel system and bridge. You start by going underground in the tunnel; then it brings you up in the middle of the highway so you see water all around you, and then brings you back down under. Norm and I just had fun driving, nothing else really mattered. When we got to Orlando and checked into the Doubletree (warm cookies!) we checked out the two suites to figure out where all of us would be sleeping. My brother and my dad met us at the hotel. It was nice because my brother and I could switch back and forth for what we wanted to do those days. I had to fly back with my father and brother because we needed to get back for school. My mom and stepfather drove back on their own.

While we were down there my great aunt passed away. Once again, the morning that the phone call came in I was the one to grab the phone before it rang. Upon answering I said hi to the correct aunt, even before she talked. Then after her hi back, I said Aunt Mariah died didn't she? To which my aunt responded yes she did. I said okay, I'll tell my mom. Have a good day.

About a week before that I had written about how amazing Great Aunt Mariah was. She was one of the strongest women I've ever met. She didn't have children of her own, so she took care of the rest of us. We always knew we had a safe place at her house.

I wrote:

She's a fighter always has been
Right now I wish she'd take the easy way out and just give up
She won't though it's not in her vocabulary
Her life's been full of pain and suffering but she always smiled
One of the family guardians
It's our time now
We have to be strong
Together the family is stronger and happier
Our love for her should be our strength
We should always remember what's stronger: blood or water.
Because of that give the benefit of the doubt to each other
Like she would.

That was written ten days before she passed. The only thing about it that sticks out is that I always felt safe when I was with her. I also remember my mother seeing her in the hospital. She kept saying no you have to fight this! You can get through it. You always do. After those comments I wrote the above letting her know it was OKAY. She had been fighting for her life for years.

With Whitey's urging I briefly dated a boy that worked with my brother at the first internet company in the area. He lived in a neighboring town and also had his license and since his family was wealthy, he had a sweet convertible. We hung out at his house mostly and did some heavy petting (yuck, when did I become so old that's the word I chose?).

It wasn't really a super important relationship other than the fact that I was already learning to only tell half-truths when it came to dating. I ended up introducing him to a friend of mine…she was kinda promiscuous looking back at it. Really? Once again feeling far too old to be writing about my thoughts as a teen, but it's important and twenty-five years ago those would have been the words we used, so? He broke up with me a couple days before the freshman/sophomore social and decided to bring her to the dance. Oops?

I really didn't care but it did allow me to have a little fun in my highly religious school. I already had a pair of tickets since you could only get couples tickets. Another close girlfriend was moving out of state before the end of the summer and hadn't planned on going to the dance originally. But since she found out it would be her last opportunity to go I asked her to be my date.

This is where the fun started—I think I may have gotten whiplash at how quickly the two of us were yanked into the principal's office. "Tickets for the dance are meant to be one girl and one boy. If you want to go without a boy you must buy two sets of tickets."

"Wait what?" I know my jaw must have dropped upon saying that, but I continued, "So you're saying that even though I have two tickets we can't use them?"

"No, you have a couples ticket. Two girls are not a couple. You are not going to make a spectacle of the school!" was the response I was given.

I wanted to continue to push it as the two of us were going as a couple. But she was from a very Catholic home and shook her head at me. So I gave in. "We are just friends and she is moving next year. Plus my boyfriend just broke up with me to take my other best friend to the dance."

We were made to promise that we were not trying to cause a scene and they let us go together…but really, were we?

This summer I mainly remember going to camp and either being a counselor or heading to Maine for Mission Camp. Maine Mission Camp stands out because it was the only time I left the actual camp for a week. The camp director's nephew (who was nineteen when I was sixteen) went with us. I remember sitting with him waiting to load the van. He was just staring at me, which caused me to get angry and ask what he was doing. He chuckled and said, "You just got mad. Your eyes change color. Now they have a ring of fire around them!" I had never noticed that my eyes change color until that moment. Nobody had told me. My mother usually focused on the fact that blue is the rarest color and mine weren't blue. Well guess what, green is actually the rarest eye color and is the only one that truly changes because of lighting reflecting to make them appear blue or have rings of fire.

We got up there and they had these nice cabins with air and showers. There weren't as many girls as boys for a change so our cabin wasn't over crowded. Michael, the friend that had gotten food poisoning, went up, as well as my brother and other friends. Both Michael and I were very picky eaters. We had much more limited meals at the campsite, so the two of us ate Corn Pops all week. I think I stopped eating Corn Pops for years after that week. It was a nice small group, maybe twelve of us total? We had so much!

We painted an elderly couple's house yellow, on probably the hottest day of the summer. Well, and ourselves? Michael and I were the two that really got painted and probably had more paint on ourselves than the house. When we got back, it was so hot that we just couldn't cool down. The director decided to bring us to a swimming hole that was under one of the oldest wire bridges in the country. It was beautiful and there was even a waterfall. When Michael and I took off our dry clothes to go in everybody started laughing because we were still covered in paint. It looked like we had yellow skin. To get it off we went under the waterfall, which of course was colder than the rest of the water since it was moving so fast. It was close to one hundred degrees out but I was shivering.

Another week of camp I was a counselor for late elementary kids in a hogan. Hogans are shelters on a wooden platform with tent-like fabric over and tie-back doors with screens. The beds were more like wooden cots with zero lighting. They were about a mile into the woods away from the solar bathhouse, and further from the dining hall, cabins, waterfront, and main retreat center.

This week was more eventful than most: a camper brought lice into one of the hogans. Luckily it was not mine. The entire hogan

Athena Tempest Rose

had to get deloused by the nurse and then everybody's clothes had to be washed. It was such a long process, especially since only staff had access to washing machines and they didn't have hot water. I'm guessing some of the staff were sent to a laundromat. I know it was horrible and long but I am glad that the child that brought the lice in made it to camp, because otherwise they were home in a horrible setting by themselves.

Yes, my hogan missed the lice; instead we had a child that was afraid to shower and had clothes that were so dirty none of the other kids or I could sleep in the hogan. The other campers were so sweet in trying to help her. They tried to buy her an outfit from the camp store. We didn't let them but did make sure she had clean clothes. Then after FOB (feet on bunks) on Monday we brought everyone down to the waterfront for swimming. As planned from talking to the camp nurse and staff, myself and another counselor brought her with us to the bathhouse while a staff member drove to our hogan to grab her clothes. Camp was the one place she felt safe so we didn't want any of the kids making fun of her. When we got to the bathhouse we sent her to a stall to shower.

For the first fifteen minutes the water ran and we thought she was showering, but she wasn't. She was shaking in fear. So the three of us got down to our bathing suits and went into the larger handicapped stall. We turned the water on and set it to a comfortable temperature. Then I put my body under the stream of water. We had her place her hand under to know that the water was a good temperature and not burning or freezing. I stepped out but stayed right next to the water and asked her to stand under it. She was shaking but stepped under. We put shampoo in her hand to scrub in her hair. I can't imagine what she had gone through because she was afraid to use it. We ended up helping every step of the way.

I wanted to help her more but I didn't know how other than what I did. It wasn't my fault. It wasn't my responsibility to fix things for her but that's the way I am. I don't want to see somebody else hurting. I never have. I never will. If it means I can be the one that gets hurt instead I will push somebody else out of the way so they don't know what pain feels like. But in this case I just couldn't.

When we returned to the other campers they were just leaving the waterfront to head to games on the grass. No one even paid attention to us being wet because they were as well. The rest of the week I had a happy camper that wanted hair brushed with the other kids and just played. Before the shower she sat off by herself.

I know I was sneaking up and seeing Whitey at this point, but I don't recall very many new memories about it, just that it continued. He would call me in. Want me to be there with him. Tell me all the bad things that ever happened. That I was his only reason for living. Then seconds later he would tell me I was trying to destroy his life. I needed to get out. I was a whore. He was disgusted by me. It was always a push and pull. It was worse now because I had lost a ton of weight, so "I was trying to get guys to notice me."

This was also the point where Whitey started noticing my bathroom issues. Due to all the "healthy eating," lots of salads and chicken and whole grain breads, I wasn't going to the bathroom at all. He decided on the best thing to do to make me go to the bathroom. That's when the enemas started. I know this is going to sound really gross and seriously, the whole world is going to know way more about me than I ever wanted by the end of this, but if it helps one person it's worth it. I can't say that my digestive tract would have been perfect if not for Whitey, because remember the kindergarten story? So yes, it just continued to get worse and worse. Whether it was genetics, being born early, the stress of feeling alone, being forced to have sex at such a young age, or being afraid to go to the bathroom...something was not working right. Well, he decided he knew how to fix me.

The first time I had no idea what was about to happen. Whitey told me to lie on the bathroom floor, ass up. Okay? I'm thinking that he's about to fuck my ass. I almost started crying at the thought. My stomach hurt something awful. How could he want to have sex with me like this? But instead I felt plastic and pressure. What the fuck? I started to cry. He told me it would make me feel better. I tried to stop the tears. At first it didn't really hurt. Until it did! I needed to get up and use the bathroom. He wouldn't let me. He literally held my ass cheeks together while I writhed in agony, trying not to cry. He held me there for a good five minutes.

11th Grade

Otherwise known as five years in

Walking into junior year of high school was different: I had friends. I looked slimmer. I was proud of my curves. I was ready to start applying for colleges. I was a "big sister" to an incoming freshman. I was an important part of the school outreach program. I had a vehicle to drive whenever I wanted to leave the house. It wasn't mine but at least it was reliable for the most part.

I finally had the space in my schedule to take drama class. I loved performing but we no longer had a full drama club which meant no performances at the school. In elementary school I had been lucky enough to play a part in five plays out of Trinity Arts Center, a feeder for Trinity Repertory. The best piece of being in drama class was I met Red. We would become best friends and referred to each other as brother and sister. I had been looking forward to plays which I remembered from when my cousin attended the high school. However, we didn't have money for it while I was there. Apparently all the extra funding went into the sports and technology programs. It's always sports, isn't it? They are never the first expense to be cut. But the kids that do well in school and want to put on a play, nope! Technology funding was important, but still.... I mean we were on the cusp of having computers but we didn't quite yet. We had word processors. We learned to type using correct finger placement and had the ability to check spelling and grammar before printing a paper. This was a huge step up from those before us.

The library was in the same building as the technology lab, perfect for researching and writing a paper if you stayed at school to do that stuff. The high school is considered a college prep school so we were all supposed to have that as our goal in life. Which meant learning to do research using books and encyclopedias and understanding how to find books using the Dewey decimal system. There was no way I was staying after every day, partly because of me and partly because I was required to drive four other kids home daily.

Instead of typing papers in school I would go to my dad's. I learned that my dad was very OCD when it came down to writing papers. After he "helped" with the first paper I learned how little work I actually needed to do. So I would give him the topic of the paper and sit next to him in front of our word processor because he could type so much faster than I could. I would have random notes for it, but since he never liked any of the ideas I came up with I literally would sit there while he wrote my entire paper. Yeah, that's a form of cheating but he just did it. The papers were done in a couple hours each. Why would I do it alone? I always got overwhelmed alone, which would mean weeks of staring at blank pages. Even worse were the days I wrote out the entire paper and just planned on going to my dad's for typing. As soon as he saw the paper he would take it out of my hand and start typing. Except what was handed back was not my paper. After that if I wanted it to be my voice, I stayed home and used a typewriter. But that meant changes caused me to have to type it all again.

By the beginning of eleventh grade I had lost all the weight that my parents and Whitey had deemed I needed to lose to be healthy for them. In tenth my dad had signed me up for Jenny Craig with him; it worked to lose the weight. However, something that was unknown in the '90s was that you needed fat in your diet to be healthy. Fats are broken down using your gallbladder. When you take fats out of your diet your gallbladder stops working. However, we can't live without any fats in our lives, so when you add it back in, that nonworking gallbladder freaks out and doesn't know what to do. For me this meant pain so severe that I was curled up on the living room floor every afternoon after school. I was barely making it through school but I had to go to school. It was the one place I knew nobody was gonna yell at me. At school I was treated like everybody else. I was safe. Which meant I went to school even though I couldn't tell you what was happening there.

Well I remembered drama class because we talked about sex all the time. Or I should say I was asked about sex all the time, because remember? My other hiding spot was the bookstores. By this time I knew I wanted to be a sexual psychiatrist so I knew how it was supposed to work. I studied how to get a guy to orgasm quickly. I researched birth control and statistics on pregnancies. I researched sexual assault. I thought sex with Whitey was the way it was supposed to be, because all the books talked about how important it was to help the male orgasm. In the 1990s everything about sex meant how guys orgasmed and girls got pregnant. Everyone talked about how much fun it was supposed to be, but at this point I was much more into just being done.

Red was probably the best part of eleventh grade. Him and I were inseparable at times. I would go to his house and watch movies. Without fail I would fall asleep on him and would wake up fully clothed on his lap with his hand on my head, nothing else. I finally had a safe place. His mom was always nice to me and invited me over whenever I wanted. In the summers I would go over to go swimming, well, until Whitey and I were living together.

This was about the same time Whitey must have been starting to feel like he wouldn't get caught and even if he did he could try to pretend he thought I was eighteen. Whitey started sneaking off with me and bringing me to parking lots and parks to have sex. Before he would park he always made sure to tell me that if a policeman comes up to the car I am to respond that I was there of my own free will. Then if they asked how old I was I needed to say I was eighteen every time. I always did as I was told for fear of learning the consequences and because I loved him and I thought this was what you did for those you loved.

By this time I was working at the candy factory as well. Which meant I had very little time to do anything out of the ordinary. I had time to work, go to school, work on homework, babysit, and drive others around. By bedtime I pretty much wanted to just climb into bed and sleep but instead I was sneaking upstairs. This probably played a role in me getting into an accident at school.

Norm had gotten a brand new truck that year. He let me drive it to school one day because he was working on the other vehicles. I really was a pretty good driver, but some things a newer driver just can't estimate as well. The day in question was a finals day, this meant for upperclassmen we could leave as soon as we were done. I had only one final that day. The parking lot was pretty tight for parking. When I went outside the two cars on either side of the truck were super tight. There was no way I was waiting two hours to leave. So I climbed in through the passenger side. Yeah, we can tell this isn't going to end well. I slowly start backing up thinking I can just clear this. All of a sudden I hear a crushing noise. Oh Fuck!!! I pull forward and adjust. Then finish backing up. I drove around the lot in a circle to see if there was any damage. I didn't see any. So I drove home. The truck is perfectly fine, maybe a slight crack in the blinker.

On Monday, I get to school and partway through the second period I hear my name over the loudspeaker: "Athena, come to the office." I have no idea why. When I get there the principal has me sit down. This is only the second time I had ever been called to his office. Fuck, what did I do? The second he starts talking

I'm like, Shit! I hit someone's car and he didn't notice when he left the school. He literally parked it in the garage with no idea I had crushed the rear quarter panel. When his dad got home from work he got in so much trouble! I thought I was going to be in so much trouble. The principal said someone saw me hit it and reported it to the boy. I said yeah that must have been me, but I drove around the lot after hitting it and looked for damage. I must have not looked close enough cause I didn't see any. The principal decided that as long as our two families could work out the problem I wasn't going to be given detention or suspension because I was honest. Norm was able to fix the car and I was taken off the insurance policy for the truck. To this day, knock on wood, I've only hit inanimate objects driving…

Speaking of driving, that winter was pretty crazy in regards to snow. We didn't have computer generated tracking systems to have them say probabilities every couple of seconds. Instead, the weather people had to go to years of school to try and guesstimate when storms would hit. These were the days of joking about how weather people had the only profession that literally could be wrong half the time and still have a job. There was one day where this stood out the most. When we went to school it was not snowing. However, the snow started picking up quickly and all the schools had to release somewhere between eleven and one o'clock. However, it was already too late. Buses were having a hard time getting kids home. Which did not bode well for me. I had four other kids in the car and had to drive them each to their house before heading home. I was driving a 1970s Plymouth Fury, which is a big boat, completely metal. We were going to be safe if I got into an accident but I didn't want to test that. However, what I didn't know was it had bald tires. Because I didn't know, I thought I just couldn't drive in the snow. Except I wasn't allowed to get my license without Norm giving me multiple trials in snow and losing control.

This particular day was going to test my driving skills. Driving home, we barely got out of the parking lot. Then there was a set of lights that turned red. I tried to stop but I just kept going, not in a straight line but into a snowbank. Then I started crying. Luckily there was a car full of college guys right next to me. They got out of the car and helped push me out of the snowbank. Safely out of the first snowbank, I keep driving. Until I see a bus, I should have plenty of time to stop. But I try to stop and I just can't come to a complete stop. The bus's red lights went on and the kids all started crossing looking at me. Then stopping in the middle while laughing. My car is still moving towards them because I cannot stop. I am frantically waving my hands and screaming. As is everybody else in my car! We are screaming at these kids to move across the street or back towards the bus but instead they decide they want to stand in front of a car that is coming towards them and laugh. Luckily I did not hit them and I finally came to a stop. Getting going again was a whole other problem. Slowly I started moving in a straight line. But crap, within a half mile I have to turn right to get down another street. I start turning and I just continue going straight. There was nothing I could do but drive straight.

I realize at this point I'm not gonna make it home with five kids. I just decided to keep going; about a mile down there was a McDonald's that hadn't quite closed yet. I managed to make it into the parking lot. Then we all went inside. Cell phones did not exist, so I begged to use their phones. I luckily got ahold of my stepfather and a buddy of his. They came and got us. But it took forever because of the snow. Once there they split up and drove two kids home each. At this point my stepfather was driving the Fury and goes "Oh yeah shit the tires are really bald. I am surprised you made it as far as you did." Well gee thanks, but it did make me feel a little better.

There was another big snowstorm before the end of the school year. It was the April Fools blizzard; literally, we had thirty inches of snow. Yes that meant we didn't have school that day. It started around eleven that night so we woke up to having had snow dumped on us. My stepfather had a plow and a few plowing jobs from the season. I went with him. We ended up spending the whole day together plowing from a blizzard that was so late in the season many had taken the plows off their trucks already; I mean the prior week was fifty- and sixty-degree weather. We of course had plenty of storage space so we had the plow on in minutes. As we drove around people were waving us down and asking how much. It was crazy and by the afternoon we were both in sweatshirts with the windows down. It was so much fun and allowed me to just be.

At the end of the school year a friend of mine was moving away. I was also scheduled to have surgery the week after school let out. I decided to have a pool party at my house for her, partly because if someone else had the party I wouldn't have been able to go. We invited all of our friends and the senior she had a crush on. He came since I asked him to, even though I didn't really know him. I mean I knew he was on the football team and a twin, but that was about it. He showed up while we were playing a game, I can't remember what it was at this point. I do know that I had ended up outside the pool. He was in the pool. I slapped his back with my hand. I learned right then that you don't slap people when they are wet. It was so loud and it immediately raised and turned beet red. I was like "Oh shit! I am so sorry!" Apparently he didn't care all that much because he liked me? I don't know why. Angela, my friend, was so mad because she had a crush on him. Apparently, he'd had a crush on me. I didn't even remember more than his name from school. Had we even really met before the party?

Of course Whitey was watching us. He was pissed when he saw Monroe kissing me. I didn't initiate it but had been rubbing my hand on his back where I had hit it and he turned and grabbed my face. We dated for a couple weeks before I had surgery and he

Reclaiming Me

had to leave for freshman football training at college. While I was in the hospital the two of us talked (when I was not vomiting) each morning for hours. When he was able to come home and work for the summer, I was finally released from the hospital, and we got to actually date. Well, that was until Whitey kiboshed it. Whitey hated football players and just wanted to control me. So he spent a lot of time tearing Monroe apart.

I don't remember the exact specifications but he worked at the movie theater and so did I. We didn't work together as far as I recall. However, we dated for most of the summer. One day we got into a conversation about school because I had friends that were telling me to watch out. I had no idea why so I asked. He then told me the story that had been going around the school. I literally have no recollection of it from school, but I was disassociating every day because of what was going on with Whitey and the rest of my trauma. I was not part of the rumor mill at all. I couldn't tell you who was whose boyfriend or girlfriend, who supposedly did this and who did that. I also wasn't a drinker or smoker. The story behind Monroe was that he apparently threatened another team's quarterback with a gun. Woah! Wait up! We live in a very blue state and barely anyone who is not law enforcement has a gun license and even less a concealed carry. So why the heck did this kid have a gun at a football game?

What he told me was that he was at his grandparents' house. His grandfather had been teaching him how to shoot and the correct way to care for a gun. They had taken it apart, cleaned it, and put it back together. There were zero bullets in the gun or in the vehicle. He thought he was being funny as a teenage boy. He was joking with a player from the other team, which turned into some choice words and making fun of each other. Monroe told the other football player that if he didn't shut up and just apologize for losing so badly, he would shoot him. I think he got suspended for two weeks from school, but not during football season. Yup! Football pretty much runs New England all of fall, so he was mainly given a slap on the wrist. We broke up when he moved onto campus for the year.

Within days of ending junior year I had gallbladder surgery. Gallbladder removal is supposed to take less than a couple hours. You were supposed to go home the same day because it's a laparoscopic surgery and usually pretty routine. I was brought to the same place my mom had her gallbladder taken out...

Mine was not routine. I was scheduled for the second or third time slot of the day but because of the fact that doctors never quite know what might happen, my surgery got pushed later and later. As it got later they said that there was a possibility that I wasn't gonna be able to go home because it was gonna be too late in the day. I remember going under and being told at that point, "If you can wake up quickly after surgery you'll be able to go home"; then I was out.

As soon as I started waking up the first thing I did was yell at myself to sit up and get moving. I need to wake up right now! You need to get moving! You need to be able to go! I barely opened my eyes. I think I see my mom, my dad, my stepfather, and my brother all standing over me waiting to see how the surgery went. I remember someone saying "You don't have to wake up, you're staying here." Um...okay, but I wanna go home!" They repeated "It's okay, go back to sleep," so I did. The next time I woke up it was about two o'clock in the morning.

I was in the surgery recovery room where there were around twenty adults all in different stages of waking up, recovering, or just waiting to be moved to an actual room. Then there was me. A seventeen-year-old who just woke up to screams of agony from adults. I was alone in a hospital bed with no idea where I was or what was going on. Luckily, one of the nurses realized I was awake and she came over to check on me. I was crying because I needed to pee but didn't know how to get up. She tried to tell me it was okay, just let it go. I was confused. I started crying more saying "I can't pee in the bed." She then explained that I had a catheter and I wouldn't be peeing in the bed. After she calmed me down a little bit, she decided it wouldn't be a bad idea to let me move around a little bit if I was stable enough to stand. I managed to get up even though it hurt like hell! I was so dizzy and started vomiting the second I sat to pee. The nurses tried to convince me to let them reinsert the catheter or at least put a pad under me, but I insisted I would be fine.

Once I was all cleaned up and back in bed, I realized I didn't know where my parents were. I was told that they went home. The nurses tried to call my mom. She didn't answer her phone. I ended up staying in the recovery room until about seven or so. The staff got me a room as early as they could. Apparently, I was not going home that day either. There were complications from the surgery. I had extra bile ducts, had coded on the table, and had a drain in.

After I was moved to a room, my mother finally visited. When I asked why nobody stayed with me my mom said that the doctor told her no one was needed. Supposedly, I wasn't going to wake up until morning. My dad said that my mother had told him not to come hours before I even went in for surgery. How did I see everybody standing around me when I woke up? According to my mom she was the only one there after surgery. She left not long after. I felt very alone. Whitey called to check on me and said he couldn't come visit but loved me.

I was still in the hospital the next day. They needed to get the vomiting down and were waiting till I passed gas to send me home. I was able to go home on the third day after I had gone twelve hours without being sick. They had been giving me fluids through my IV, so I just didn't eat to get to leave the hospital. Once home I quickly became dehydrated. I couldn't go to the bathroom or keep food down. My dad brought me back to the hospital. They did a bunch of tests, gave me more fluids, but still couldn't figure out what was wrong. So they sent me back home again about two days later.

I must have been too much work for my mom, so she had my dad pick me up as he was moving into his new place. It was the end of June and pretty hot out. I couldn't help with the move and there was nothing in the new house yet, so he left me in the car with the windows down. How was I going to stay there with him? It was so hot and I couldn't go anywhere. I started getting sick again. I'm so sick, I'm shaking and unable to keep sips of water down. The pain was so bad I was curled in a ball. My dad got an area set to bring me inside with an air conditioner. I really don't know any other details of the day, other than he didn't let me sleep alone. He was afraid I would choke on my own vomit. I don't know which night it was—it could have been the first night there or days later—but he wasn't going to allow me to just keep getting sicker. He brought me back to the hospital again. This time they did even more tests.

If you have a weak stomach you may want to skip this part. One of the tests required me to drink barium. I tried drinking it. It came right back up. This test they felt was the one that would answer what was going on. So they need the barium down. Since I couldn't drink it, a feeding tube was placed down my throat. Then the nurse tried to push the barium through. Apparently I am super special because suddenly the barium starts coming back up the feeding tube. After talking to the doctors, the nurses decided it was okay. I was going to be sent to imaging with the barium, and it would be pushed there. We got this figured out. But then they decided that the staff member for moving me to imaging was a cute eighteen-year-old boy. He walks in while I'm walking out of the bathroom with my ass in view thanks to the johnny. He gets me all set sitting up in the bed while he walks. The nurses have the feeding tube down my nose. There is barium coming out of it. And the kid was flirting with me. I'm not sure if I've been more embarrassed in my life. But I mean why was he flirting with me? I had a feeding tube and stuff coming out of my nose!

This was just the test we needed. They found out that I was full of shit, literally. My intestines hadn't woken up from surgery. The reason why everything was coming right back up was because it couldn't go down. Luckily, barium is super heavy; it managed to push some of the impaction down. The nurses also started enemas. Within twenty-four hours of fluids and enemas I was sent home. This was two weeks after having my gallbladder surgery. I was finally doing better. But I was sent to a gastroenterologist to figure out why my body doesn't work like a normal human's. I was pretty much sick that entire summer. I couldn't counsel at camp, because the one week I tried I had to go home Monday because of pain and vomiting.

Since I was going into my senior year I had my senior pictures taken. When we got the proof my mom said I looked like I was a drug addict. So she called the photographer and told them just that. She had them do retakes. Over the summer Whitey pushed enemas every week. Each time I lay on his bathroom floor crying till he let me up. But I was sure he was helping so it was okay. I did NOT want to end up back in the hospital.

Finally a Senior...

Which also meant I was legally an Adult

As senior year was about to start I realized just how few friends I still had. I hadn't been allowed sleepovers, I wasn't allowed to attend school events (except for the big ones to keep others from noticing), or pretty much do anything other than go to school. Whitey was controlling everything I did and for some reason my mother didn't seem to care. Is it possible she didn't know? It seems highly doubtful. Very recently I was able to speak to someone else that was around but really didn't have any say in how to raise me. They had been told that I was only spending time with Whitey for homework help. Why don't I remember that conversation at all? There is pretty much zero chance that's what my mother thought. Every time I write more I get upset more, wondering just what I did so wrong that my mother didn't care about me.

Alright, back to my story...

Senior year and I barely know or remember anyone in my class. There was a friend of mine that had died over the summer. She had cancer. We thought she was finally coming back to school. But there was an infection and she was too weak to fight it. The wake was full of kids from school. I went and felt completely alone. Those that had been my friends I hadn't talked to since before school ended. I was still sick and hadn't been allowed to hang out. Would I ever be normal?

However, I was super excited starting senior year. I thought

Reclaiming Me

that everything was gonna all work out and be better this year. I was about to turn eighteen which meant that I could legally be with Whitey and everything was perfect. Or so I thought. Apparently for my birthday my stepfather and my mother decided that they would run cable to my bedroom. However, I don't know what happened on my actual birthday; when I came home from school my stepfather and I got into a huge fight. I'm guessing it was probably something about Whitey but I honestly don't remember. I could probably ask him but I feel like my non-memory of it may be a good thing. After that fight I was so upset I tried to talk to my mother, which of course went badly, and she told me I could leave and I wasn't allowed to take a vehicle.

So I've got my backpack with all my school stuff and still had my school uniform on with a pair of sneakers. This meant I was in a plaid skirt and a button-down shirt. I started walking to my grandmother's apartment, it was around five miles. I used all back roads because it was more direct that way, otherwise it might've been a six- to eight-mile walk. I walked by the scene of the accident my brother had. It felt like a little piece of my history falling away. I had to just keep walking till I got to my grandma's. I can't even count how many guys drove by in their pickup trucks beeping, pulling over, screaming lewd comments out of their windows, calling me sexy, or offering me rides. It made me wrap my arms further around my body, push my skirt as low as possible to cover my legs more, and cry as I walked. I didn't want to be looked at. They made me feel like a piece of meat. I walked and cried thinking that no one would ever love me.

Luckily my grandmother was perfectly happy to see me. We didn't talk at all that night. She just made dinner and helped me put clean sheets on my bed. My grandmother had a spare bedroom in her apartment and had set it up mainly for me because I stayed over the most. So it came as no surprise that she was happy with me moving in, at least temporarily. I went to school and went back to my grandma's house. I didn't talk to my mother for a while. After a few weeks at my grandmother's place I then moved in with my dad. By this time my brother was in college and living on campus. So my dad set me up in his room. There were only two bedrooms at the time so my dad had a bedroom and living room put in the basement for my brother. Not long after I moved in with my dad he had to go to South Carolina for work. Which meant I was living at the house alone for the next couple months.

I turned eighteen at the beginning of senior year. This meant that businesses didn't have to let me leave early to get to school the next day because I was eighteen. It didn't matter that I was a senior in high school. I worked the closing shift at the movie theater. During the release of Titanic. If you're too young to know what that means, think about the most popular movie you know and realize that the only way to see that movie is in a theater, now multiply that by ten and you'll understand the chaos that was caused. The lines to get popcorn and other concessions would run around fifty people deep. I literally didn't stop ringing people up until about thirty minutes into the last showing of the night. Which meant we would clean up everything and then finally go home or just go sit in the back row of Titanic. I can't tell you how many times I passed out watching it. The worst part though was when I got home all I smelt was popcorn and I even dreamt about it. I literally couldn't touch popcorn for a year after because all I could think of was that smell and the layer of grease on my clothes, hair, and face.

While I was working at the movie theater I met Pags. Pags was a few months younger than me so he was still seventeen. We were both seniors in high school. We started dating. We ran on high intensity all the time, which is very typical in high school relationships. It's the time in your life where everything is based on a need now principle and not how it will affect your future. We would skip school just to go to my house and have sex, or head there after work on weekends. I was still sick from complications of the surgery and whatever autoimmune disorder I have. With my doctor's note confirming ongoing health problems I could stay home whenever I was having a bad day.

I definitely used my medically excused absences more than they were needed. Which is why it really wasn't much of a surprise when I failed senior English. Not only was I not going to school all the time but I also just didn't write my papers. The papers were not missed because I was skipping school, but instead because I was disassociating and also had undiagnosed ADHD. I also wasn't just dating Pags, Whitey was also coming over on school days when my dad was working in South Carolina. Plus it was before video chats and cell phones, so the only way to know what someone was doing was really showing up. Needless to say I had a lot of sex that year. When Whitey was over it was more to check that I wasn't doing anything with anyone else…Yes, I got really good at lying. I mean he told me to have a boyfriend and then once I did and told him he beat me to the point where I stayed home for a week just so no one would ask questions. I also told Pags I had a flu and he couldn't come over.

I knew I was having sex and that Whitey refused to use protection, but that wasn't acceptable to me so I went to Planned Parenthood and was put on the pill. I had been on it before I moved in with my dad, so as soon as I moved in I placed it on the kitchen counter for a month. He didn't say anything but it was obvious he knew that I was trying to protect myself. My dad couldn't have these conversations at all. As I got older I worked for him in two places as an assistant controller. It was his responsibility; in being the controller of a small company he also had to do office manager-type things. Which meant he was responsible for making sure everything was cleaned and whatnot in the building. Making sure that women had pads, tampons, and anything else we might need in the bathroom was his responsibility. Seeing as how they were small offices, having a coin controlled one wasn't an option. It was put on me to get a little box and keep it stocked. I loved trying to hand him the boxes with the receipt to put in petty cash and he would look at me and say "Nope, nope, nope"; then push them to me and walk away.

Okay, back to failing. I failed senior English which meant that I wasn't gonna graduate unless I fixed it. I had already applied and was accepted to every college I had applied to. I had also applied for scholarships. I was trying to figure out how to make college more affordable. Then out of nowhere I got a letter in the mail from a school I had never replied to telling me I had a free ride. Yeah really, I got a letter from a Catholic university telling me I didn't have to pay anything to go to school. The offer included living on campus, books, and food. I would be crazy to give that up!

You might ask, why would I get a full scholarship? Well, from the time I can remember I have volunteered for everything and anything I could. In high school I volunteered as Santa's elf for the school's Christmas gift program. The school took toy and other gift donations for about a month leading up to right before Christmas. It's a pretty amazing sight as everyone moves the gifts out to vehicles from the school. We line up shoulder to shoulder and make a human conveyer belt to pass the gifts. They are then driven to the church where the program would allow parents to shop for their children while we kept the kids occupied to keep the presents a surprise. Santa, his elf, and other students were set up in an enclosed part of the church with the kids to color, play games, and to ask Santa for presents. I would help Santa by helping the kids to be comfortable and listening in on the conversation since sometimes it meant I would have to excuse myself and find parents to help them shop.

I also volunteered at a local nursing home for part of middle school and all of high school. While there I got to learn about the

Roaring Twenties, Prohibition, the Great Depression, and World War II from those that lived it. Some of my volunteering didn't even strike me as work, like going to the senior center with my grandmother. I loved going and would play cards and chat with them, but the director would grab me and have me pass out drinks and food or clean up areas as needed, as well as help people get around.

The "Santa Shop" was not the only volunteering I did at school, just the one that was most noticeable. I also volunteered at camp as a counselor. I pretty much wanted to help people at all times. Which shouldn't be too surprising based on the fact that I'm writing to help people understand what grooming looks like and how to heal from it.

The college that sent me a free ride was in New York. I badly wanted to get away from home. Which meant the decision to go to this school was an easy one. However, I almost lost it. I needed to get that English grade to passing! Which meant I lost my free period for the second semester. Which meant I could no longer leave the building during my free period because I needed a tutor. The tutor, who was a new teacher, would have me sit in a freshman study hall and write my papers during the study hall. She would then have me hand them in to her. By the end of it she looked at me and said, "Seriously, if you had just passed these in on time even if they were handwritten you wouldn't have failed." So yeah, I'm stubborn, and since my work wasn't exactly as the teacher had said it needed to be I just didn't pass it in.

Towards the end of the year I quit the movie theater and started working at Claire's, because the late nights were just too much. Claire's was pretty good. It was only a few people working at a time. I quickly became the assistant manager because I was good with money, numbers, and had an eye for setting up the store. It was pretty easy most of the time except for on the weekends. We would have to open both registers and have extra people on to help pierce ears, because when you have a little kid you do them at the same time. It was a fun job that didn't require a lot of thinking on my part.

While my dad was gone he had hidden money around the library/office in our house. We had bookshelves covering two walls and part of the third. The third also was where we kept our new computer. It took up the entire desk and the space underneath. The fourth wall was unusable because it was the space connecting our kitchen to our living room, there were no doors. Once a week my dad would call and tell me where he had hidden a hundred bucks, so I could go buy food for the week, and if needed put gas in my car. He ended up gone for more than two months once. I started running out of money. Then I started getting bills that had to be paid. He had paid ahead but two months meant we were getting new bills. At that point I had a checking account so I paid the bills. Yes, when my dad found out he paid me back, but that's what I did. I was pretty much responsible for keeping the house in usable condition by myself. I feel that I showed up to school and on time more than most high school seniors would if they were living alone.

Pags and I were very emotionally driven. The two of us had amazing chemistry and had fun together. Except, I did get triggered quite a bit, and neither one of us realized it at the time. When he came over and we had sex we would then fall asleep. Quite a few times I would wake up with no clothes on but couldn't remember anything from the time he came over till waking up next to him. The days Whitey would come over were much more problematic. Pretty much every time he came over he would immediately have me strip to "feel his property," but he was actually inspecting my body to make sure I hadn't been fucking around. Then he would get himself a drink and bring me into the bathroom for an enema. Always the same process, and always stated as him taking care of me.

Once Thanksgiving rolled around my dad and my brother came

Reclaiming Me

home for a little while. Which was also about the time Whitey stopped talking to me. He said it was because I apparently didn't need him since "I had a boyfriend" and "he might as well go date someone else." For me that was another "Okay! I am not good enough." But it also meant I was able to enjoy the rest of my senior year as a high schooler. Except most of the damage was already done. I was still scared of doing anything other than work, school, and hanging out at my house. Pags and his friends smoked and drank, but even if I would go over for a party I didn't participate in smoking or drinking. I also came up with excuses for most parties because in my head I wasn't allowed to go to them. Also, why had Whitey told me we would end up together and then just leave me?

I needed to figure out where I belonged but for now I was just enjoying the ride with Pags. We went to senior prom for my school and then a week later it was Pags's school. We had so much fun at the afterparties. For Pags's school we were able to go back to his parents' house and he had invited some good friends of his. Except, that night his best friend broke up with his girlfriend so the three of us had a threesome, but in actuality it was really me being put in between the two of them doing what they wanted to me but never touching each other. It was not what everyone fantasizes about and pretty much was over as soon as I got each of them off. Whitey had made sure I did that well.

After graduation I worked all summer at Taco Bell and Claire's running back and forth with very little sleep. I was working so much that one day when I was running from Claire's to Taco Bell I had to stop at my house for part of my uniform. That doesn't seem like a big deal especially since I usually drove right by my house to go that way. Except this particular day I literally closed my eyes when I hit the driveway and moved our concrete stairs to our porch just a little. I was working too much and playing too much. I continued to date Pags and Whitey. The only difference was nobody knew I was dating Whitey. We would meet at my house or in a parking lot. Then I would come back home and no one else even questioned where I was.

Whitey on the other hand knew where I was 24/7. He knew I was dating Pags and wanted me to continue to keep up appearances. Sometimes he would yell at me and call me horrible names because of it. Other days he would make me park in the nearby school parking lot and walk to his apartment. Those were the days Whitey would give me enemas. After them I would curl up on the bathroom floor and just stay there till he made me dinner. If I tried to get up too soon before dinner was ready I would pass out and end up on the floor anyway. Sometimes he would make me curl up in the shower because I didn't smell good so I'd crawl there and wait for him.

I was still dating Pags but Whitey didn't allow me to tell Pags I was still seeing him too. I just kind of fudged things a bit when Pags would ask questions. Luckily I was getting ready to head off to New York so Pags just thought I was shopping and preparing to leave home. This was the school that I never even applied to, but couldn't wait to start! My dad and I bought me a "woody station wagon" since it would be easy to fill with everything for college and allow me to pick up my roommate on the way to school.

Off to College...

Starting school in New York

The college I went to looked like a castle. Every time I would come on campus I would imagine seeing a horse and carriage bringing the princess. Then a prince riding up on his horse to save her from anyone that might cause her harm. On either side of the entrance were classroom buildings, the cafeteria, dorms, the administrative building, and a grassy quad. At the time it was an all-girls school except for nursing. The boys that took nursing had to stay in a dorm slightly off campus. We actually had a visitor's house which was where any boys that visited had to sleep. Being on campus with only females was overwhelming to say the least. One of the first things to happen was all of us syncing up to each other's menstrual cycles. Then we also had issues because roommates were constantly arguing over who's dating who. This was the first time I started noticing guys gravitating towards me. To this day I don't really underrstand why.

For me the scariest part of college was my first roommate. She was nice and we got along well at first, even to the point of buying matching bedding, but then it got interesting. At the beginning of spring semester we were having some issues and so were other friends. We decided the best course of action would be to switch rooms. She stayed in our room and I moved basically across the hall to a bigger room with less niceties. Not long after I switched rooms my original roommate went crazy. She swore her new roommate and others were trying to kill her so she kept knives under her pillow.

Reclaiming Me

Freshmen arrived to campus mid-August, which was earlier than the resr of the school. I guess that is somewhat normal to let them get acquainted with the school. However, we had to be there two weeks early. The first couple days we moved into our dorms and had little team building exercises all prepping us to take buses south to go to camp. It was a requirement for the freshman girls to go. I was excited because I love all types of camping. The other girls though? A huge chunk were inner-city, like the Bronx and other parts of New York. Most of them had never been camping in their lives. They had no idea what to pack or what to expect. I packed a bathing suit, comfy clothes, sneakers, a pair of flip-flops, my toiletries, books, and a notebook. Most of the others had dresses and heels, many didn't have bathing suits or know how to swim. As we loaded the buses you could see the difference between those of us from more suburban places and those from cities.

I know the hope of this week was to bring us together as a class instead of pointing out the glaring differences, but it just doesn't work that way. We were staying in cabins. The cabins had a fan, two showers, toilets, and limited lights. In my cabin I quickly became the leader since so many were freaking out about spiders being in the cabin. I told them we want the spiders because they keep the mosquitos at bay. One of the girls screamed and ran outside saying she was not sleeping with spiders. I apologized for freaking her out, then chuckling I cleared a couple of the spider webs and deposited a few daddy long legs outside. On the second day we were shown the pool; it was kinda green and had a few frogs in it. You would have thought that the frogs were going to attack us the way people were screaming. I was in hysterics laughing. I had been trying to hold it in, but come on, little green frogs? They aren't scary. After I could breathe again I saved them from the frogs. Even though I couldn't stop laughing most of the weekend I made a bunch of friends helping them get through something they were a little scared of. It was a fun trip even though we didn't get to swim quite as much as most of us would have liked.

After our team building exercises at camp we were brought back to campus. This was still a couple days before everybody else got there. I think it was Thursday or Friday. Everybody else I believe started arriving on Sunday for classes to start on Tuesday.

On Friday night there was a hurricane coming up the coast. We had a lot of wind and thunderstorms. Electricity got knocked out, but luckily it wasn't for long. It was such a muggy night that our room quickly became sticky without the AC. I love storms so I just grabbed a window seat and just zoned into the storm.

Starting college I was a psychology major. I can't remember ever wanting to be something besides a psychologist most of my life. Part of the reasoning was because I wanted to understand what had happened to me as a child. I didn't relate anything that happened with Whitey until very recently, thinking that all my trauma was from being raped at nine. I needed to know how the body reacts to sexual stimuli and how our brains change the way we see it because of what's happened to us. To me it was absolutely fascinating. I also dreamt about starting a retreat or farm for kids that had been through sexual assault or child abuse. I am hoping that I can finally reach that dream in the next few years. I want the chance to reach the kids that most of society has already written off.

Heading into college Pags and I knew we would have to work hard to keep our relationship going. We thought we could defy the odds, well he did. I knew that Whitey had other ideas. But I loved Pags. He lived at home for college and went to a college in Rhode Island I was trying to give us the best possible chance by scheduling my classes to start at nine Monday morning and then finishing at eleven Thursday morning. This meant I could go home pretty much every weekend. It was pretty great at first but then we started growing apart. Or at least that's what I can remember, but Whitey was in my ear more than anyone else. It came as little surprise that Pags and I broke up before Christmas of our freshman year.

One weekend in November I drove straight to Pags. I knew we had been growing in different directions, and I was keeping a secret from him. I mean I had pushed Whitey away and told him I loved Pags but Whitey kept telling me this was the plan. I was his, there was no way he'd let me go. Just him telling me I was his would get me aroused. I loved Pags but he wasn't a caregiver for me and I needed that...or at least that's how I felt at the time. In a relationship a caregiver tends to take care of the other person. Whitey would remind me to drink water, take my meds, buy me food, wash, fold, and put away my clothes, as well as knowing what I was doing at all times.

This weekend in particular Pags and I wanted very different things. Before college Pags enjoyed smoking weed and drinking Sambuca when he would hang out with friends occasionally. This Thursday I drove straight to him. When I got to him he was already super stoned and made me drive us to a friend's "party." We got there and it was just a group of his friends drinking and smoking. I needed out. Which meant we got into a huge fight because "I wasn't being respectful of his needs." Really? WTF? I couldn't breathe in the house so I stormed out. By the time I got in my car I was in hysterics. I drove back to my dad's house and called Whitey. I was hoping we could see each other. However, Whitey was also dating someone else "to keep up appearances." I just broke down in tears.

I didn't know what to do so I called the dorms and my roommate was like, if you come back we can go to New Jersey, right over the line. I asked what was in New Jersey. She said that her boyfriend was and he lives with a bunch of his buddies. I wasn't sure I wanted that type of company but I did need a distraction from my dumpster fire. However, it sounded like it could be fun. A group of college guys and a group of college girls hanging out, what could go wrong?

She had said, "Let's go hang out with these guys right over the line in New Jersey. I'm dating one of them and he lives with his buddies in a brownstone. They asked me to bring a few friends for the night." Looking back I can see the red flags, but I didn't understand them at the time. I didn't even think to ask how old these guys were or how long she'd been "dating" this guy.

Well, I figured why stay in the dorm and cry when you can go to a bachelor pad and laugh at the silliness that was sure to unfold with my roomies? I started driving and the traffic in the Lincoln Tunnel was horrific! My car started overheating, smoke billowing out the hood, and I'm thinking "Oh Shit, we are in The Stand!" and when were the zombies coming to eat me? If you haven't read or seen The Stand by Stephen King you should. One more red flag for the night, but nope, I make it to the gas station directly outside the tunnel, I pour coolant in, and get back in the car to finish the drive.

Upon arriving at the brownstone I find out she's never met these guys before. They met in either a chat room on AOL, or he randomly called dorm numbers till he got someone to talk to him. The college's dorm phone numbers all started with the same first four numbers out of a seven-digit phone number.

I remember these guys being hot, but I could be wrong because I had never smoked pot and had no clue what a fishbowl was at the time. It is highly likely my innocent self got stoned for the first time and never realized it. I was also an emotional mess, because Pags and I were "supposed to make it" and had just broken up in some grand form. From their place we went to a local bar that didn't check identification, which is good since the three of us were eighteen or nineteen. I may have had one drink but I definitely was not drunk. After a while we went back to the brownstone, everyone else wanted to get drunk and party. I just wanted to sleep. Somehow the hot guy that my friend was supposedly dating decided he wanted me, and I ended up in his bed. I remember waking up the next

Reclaiming Me

morning, next to him in his button-down white shirt and nothing else. I don't remember any other details of the night. I felt dirty and gross and just wanted to get home.

My car was not going to make it back to the dorms and the guys didn't drive. Luckily mass transit was something many people used in the area. Which meant to get back to school we had to take a bus from New Jersey into Grand Central Station and then the train to the college. On the way back my friends were talking about how great of a time they had, as well as saying how unfair it was that I'd gotten the hottest one of the group. I kept thinking how much I wished it hadn't been me. Especially since I had to go back the following weekend to get my car from the repair guy. Which meant going back to the guys' house to get my keys. I was freaking out but couldn't tell anyone. I brought one of my friends with me and somehow managed not to get stuck in a room with him alone.

At the time it happened, other than being afraid of the male I didn't even think to tell anyone because if Whitey found out he might literally kill the guy and it would have been my fault. Plus, I knew Whitey would have hit me and reminded me I was his slut and couldn't do anything without his permission. I also wasn't positive about what happened. We might have just slept in the same bed together. Or he could have had sex with me. I was so mad at myself for apparently being 'too intoxicated' to remember. I should have seen the flags but my life had become a maze of misguided and hurtful relationships. I didn't know exactly what happened that night, but the way he wanted me to go back to his room and acted like he owned me afterwards gave me a good sense of what may have happened.

My inability to remember what happened means I was unable to give consent. Whether he had just removed my clothes and given me his shirt to wear or had sex with me, neither was acceptable. This encounter was not consensual and is a far too common occurrence in colleges. We must teach our children, especially our sons, that they need to ask for consent, and when someone is drunk or high they cannot give consent. Anything other than an enthusiastic yes should be treated as a no.

After the car broke down my dad got me a cell phone so I could have a way to contact someone if my car ever died again. I was one of the first kids in my school to have a cell phone. Yes, I really am that old; we didn't grow up with cell phones. However, I am not complaining. For my generation if you made a fool out of yourself it usually just hung around through conversations. Now everyone and their brother will know when you make a mistake because someone without fail will be recording on their phone.

My scholarship included the requirement of work-study, and I also got paid a small amount for spending money. My work-study was homework help at the library. One afternoon I got to be the one that had to explain to a child what a period was. Luckily her big sister was upstairs, but I had to do the majority of the explanation. She was wearing overalls and was in hysterics when she got to the library that day.

I asked, "What's going on?"

She responded, "Can you come with me to the bathroom?"

"Okay, I can do that."

We went to the bathroom and as soon as we got inside she said, "I think I'm dying."

"What do you mean?" was my response.

With wide eyes she responds, "There is blood in my underwear!"

"Ah...you are not dying. You just got your period. Do you know anything about it?"

She just shook her head no.

I was trying not to explain more than I needed to, so I said, "Every female gets what we call a period once a month as we get older. No one really likes it but we have to live with it." I was only nineteen and she was not my child so I wanted her not to be scared but also not end up explaining the whole sex talk. I handed her a pad and we went upstairs to find her sister, that's where the high school kids were.

After Pags and I broke up, and then the whole incident with the guys in New Jersey, I started staying on campus during the weekends. My roommate went out most weekends and I stayed in. One night I got a phone call on the dorm phone. Remember the phone numbers all started with the same four digits. This call came in and I don't know who he was calling for, just that it ended up being a wrong number. Except, we ended up talking for hours into the night. Talking to Matthew became an emotional escape for both of us. Over the course of the next three years we got to know each other better than I knew myself. I cared about Matthew very much. He was the only one I talked to about things with Whitey. We had plans to meet a couple times but it never ended up working out.

Not long after that Whitey and I started living together when I wasn't at school. I moved in with him during winter break. Except not in his original apartment, but the second floor which was bigger. This was also right around the time my mom and Norm moved out of state. So I went to school and started driving home again every weekend. I didn't stay at school on weekends because I wasn't allowed to do much other than go to class and study. Being home meant I was doing schoolwork, cleaning and organizing the house, and making food for Whitey and sometimes the whole fire department.

I want to sit here and give you more details of that year or even that summer but I don't have them. It's one of those many things when I just can't grasp what happened. I know he was working two jobs: the firefighting which was twenty-four-hour shifts, and landscaping as needed. I also was going to school, and then home working for the summer. But that is all I can remember that first year.

When I went back for sophomore year, I was really excited.

However, as the year started it got convoluted very quickly. My birthday, like I've said, is the beginning of September so it's always been right around the start of school. Whitey came down to New York for my birthday. He got a hotel room. Then complained about how expensive the hotel rooms were in New York all weekend long. Matthew the wrong number guy was supposed to meet me on my birthday at school. If he had shown up with purple roses for me, life would have been different. He didn't and Whitey did.

We walked around the city that day looking at jewelers. He was asking me what ring I liked then kept putting them away as "too expensive." I didn't know why it mattered since it was just looking. However, the last place we went after I tried one on he told the cashier to hand him the box since I was going to keep the ring on. I looked at him confused, and the cashier said congratulations. I just sat and stared. I don't think I had a clue what to say. Was this a proposal? And was I ready? I don't think so but I would never think to embarrass Whitey so I put on a smile.

He went back home. I continued the semester at school. November 5 I get a phone call telling me there was this huge fire back home; it was Whitey's mom. She was letting me know he was at it and she was worried. The building ended up being a total loss and he hurt his knee during the fire. There was another fire in Worcester, on December 3, 1999; this one a factory burnt to the ground and six firefighters died. They had a major funeral honoring the firefighters. People from all over the state and other firehouses all came out to show their support. This meant that there were buses and huge parking lots plus lots of walking. Whitey required me to be there and had me pushing him in a wheelchair for the march. I only went back to campus to finish exams and get my stuff. Whitey had decided his fiancée needed to live and go to school at home.

The funeral itself was awe-inspiring. We all walked from the church to the cemetery. It made a person remember the danger firefighters put themselves in to help others. It also made the firefighters themselves reassess their potential sacrifice. The factory had long been closed but because there were people "squatting" in it the firefighters went in to clear it.

As soon as I went back home I lost a huge part of myself. Whitey now controlled everything I did and said. He had me change majors and go to Johnson and Wales instead of a liberal arts college because he didn't want me becoming a psychologist. I was afraid all the time. As well as having zero time to myself, which kind of started making everything spin in circles.

What Next?

My story is nowhere near complete. As I try to look back at what happened during the next few years I can see every line in his pristine "hospital corners" sheets and the colors of the walls and linoleum. What blurs are the individual moments or the times he dragged me across the floor, then rug, and bent me over the bed to inspect my vagina after I had been a "slut" at school. But over time I got out and that's the important part.

As far as my mother goes I continue to struggle with where I should go from here. I know that every time I try to talk to her about my experiences she brings up my father raping her. In my head, that means that I was a product of rape. Therefore, I'm unloved, unwanted, and a second-class citizen. I know intellectually that my self-worth is skewed but I don't know how to stop the feelings yet. But writing helps.

Remember your life is yours! You deserve to be loved and respected for who you are! I am constantly evolving so follow my accounts to see what I'm up to next. Over forty years of living for others leaves me ready to live for myself and my children. So this could get interesting...

Yes!!! Lifestyle, specifically dominant/submissive relationships, is a "loving, nurturing, intimate form of human contact and play." For those of us that have experienced abuse, suffer from depression, or anxiety being able to dictate what is going to happen allows us to feel safe.

Sounds good right? But what do I mean? And what is Lifestyle? Continue hanging out with me and/or follow me on social media to hear more. I love helping others and helping myself so any questions email me athena@athenatempestrose.com or type #athenasstorm to follow my social media.

"She wore her battle scars like wings, looking at her you would never know that once upon a time she forgot how to fly."

—*Nikki Rowe*

Appendix

There are dozens of grounding techniques. I have attached two commonly used ones and my grounding bag and its use. The grounding bag can be used with any other method or alone but is my go-to for full trigger/dissociation. All of the methods can be done alone if you are anxious or panicking in a car, at night, etc. However, if this trigger happened mid-scene, part of care should include grounding.

Breathing is a major part of grounding. I suggest holding an object or just sitting. tart with breathing in from your stomach for a count of three and out from your nose. Feel the chair or the object in your hand and repeat the breathing three times. Then use a grounding technique.

Cognitive Awareness Technique

This method uses facts that we should all know about ourselves and the world around us. I tend to compare this one to the questions asked during a concussion check. It works because the focus is on breathing and reminding ourselves what is here and now.

Remember to start with breathing in from your abdomen and out through your nose. Any or all of these questions can be asked:
1. Where am I?
2. What is today?
3. What is the date?

Athena Tempest Rose

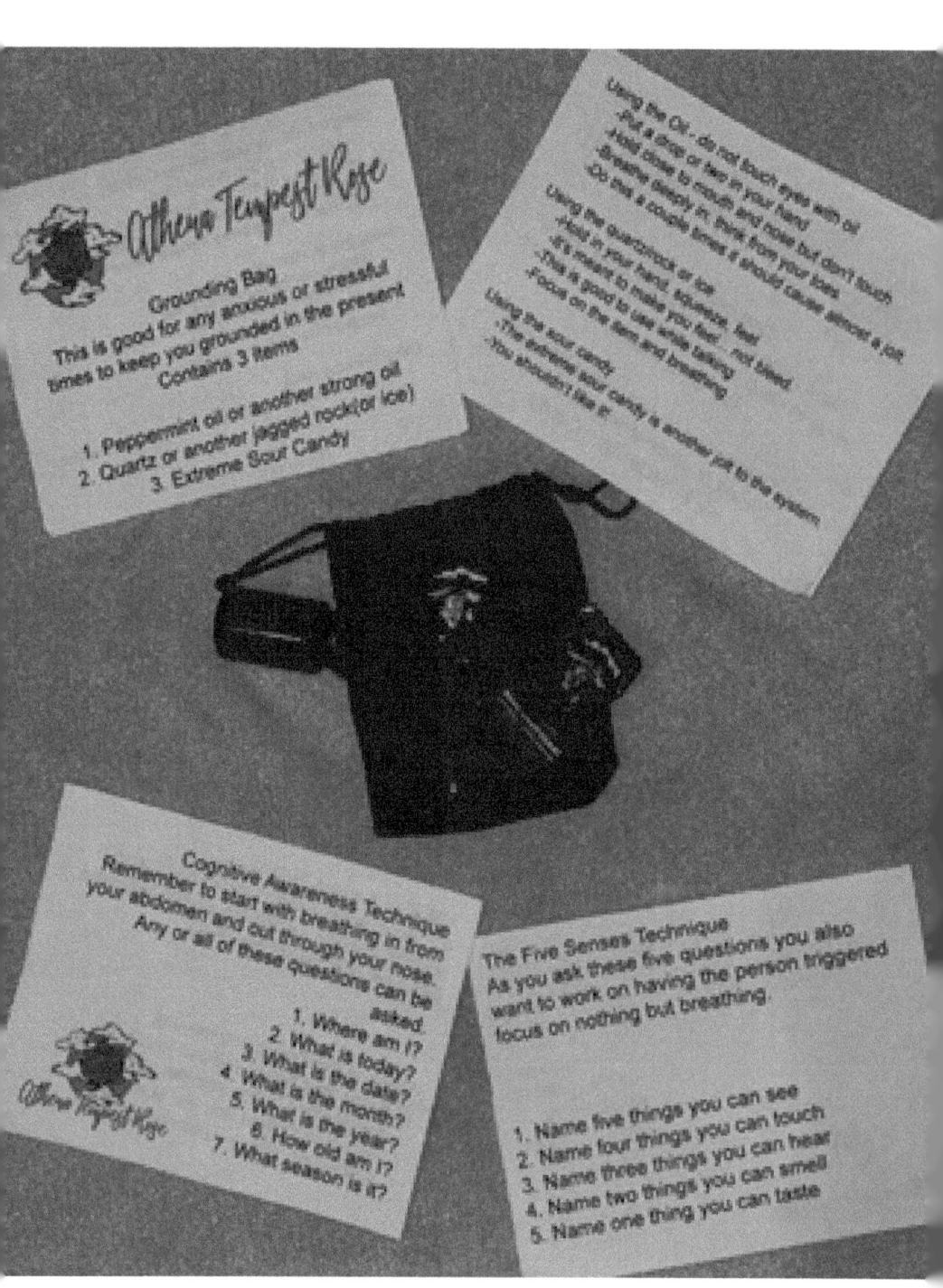

4. What is the month?
5. What is the year?
6. How old am I?
7. What season is it?

The Five Senses Technique

I love using this one as I talk through breathing with a person and can use it just as easily on the phone as I can in person. It is easy to remember and use because it's just taking something we have learned over and over and using it to ground us. It doesn't really matter which sense you use for which number; however, if you use taste for five things you might get stuck.

As you ask these five questions you also want to work on having the person triggered focus on nothing but breathing.

First, say "breathe with me" and take a deep breath in and out slowly.

Next, you ask these questions slowly and calmly. As the triggered person answers, keep the breathing slow and measured:

1. Name five things you can see.
2. Name four things you can touch.
3. Name three things you can hear.
4. Name two things you can smell.
5. Name one thing you can taste—if you have a small piece of chocolate or gum, etc., place it in your mouth before answering.

Grounding Bag

The grounding bag was taught to me by my trauma therapist, for when I can't think or breathe. It's when the C-PTSD anxiety makes it so I'm not me and can't communicate.

The bag can be used by either a person being triggered or someone witnessing the trigger.

This is good for any panic attack or stressful time period to keep you grounded in the present:

1. Peppermint oil or another overpowering oil
2. Quartz or another jagged rock (or ice)
3. Extreme sour candy

Using the oil (be careful not to touch your eyes if you have oil on your fingers):
1. Put a drop or two in the triggered person's hand.
2. They rub it in then place their hands close to their mouth and nose, but not touching.
3. They breathe in deeply, think from your toes.
4. Do this a couple times it should cause almost a jolt.
5. If you want to put it on your hands and have them breathe that's fine.

Using the quartz/rock or ice:
1. The quartz or another ragged, rough rock is for squeezing tightly in their hands.
2. Ice works just as well if not better in some cases.
3. It won't feel good. It's meant to make them feel—not bleed.
4. This is good for a mid-scene trigger since they have someone to direct what comes next.
5. As they do the talking and breathing exercises this will help them come back to the present and things are okay.

Using the sour candy:
1. The extreme sour candy is another jolt to the system.
2. You shouldn't like it!

Graphic Writings

Included as pictures above

March 30, 1995

He thinks he can just waltz in anytime he feels like it and I'll jump.
Well the jumping isn't happening anymore,
'cause my love isn't a bottomless pit that never ends.
It is a give and take situation.
I give, he takes, that's not how love works either.

May 9, 1995

I see him walking down the hall
My heart starts beating a mile a minute
My mouth dries up like a cotton ball
I can't help but look as he stops
And I can't seem to think of anything
But how much I'd like to tell him "I love you."
The only problem is my heart's been broken into tiny pieces.
And I can't help but wonder will he help or just hurt me more?

The fear etched in my heart. Never to let go until I know for certain not all guys are cruel enough to destroy a person's life. I only wish that day would come when my heart will be as free as a bird. When I will not have to hide any of my feelings; instead I can run freely telling of my feelings for him.

His smile makes my heart jump into my throat.
His face makes me want to take it and kiss it and never let it go.
His body makes my whole body scream for joy.
Then I come to the realization that I can never have him till my

heart repairs itself from the many hurts that my young life has gone through.
And I think if only I could go back to before and live life to its fullest.

Is he really that insensitive
To destroy her heart
Even after she laid it on the line
Just to find he could care less
He didn't even bother to acknowledge her
All he did was pretend it never happened
That she never tried to know him
She doesn't know if she can ever face him.
If he doesn't love her why should she
She'd only be hurt again.
Right?

Love, is it Always there?
Does it leave when times are hard?
Is it Everlasting?
Does it have limits?
Is it Joyful?
Does it cause Sorrow?
Is it Caring?

About the Author

Athena lives in New England with her four children, ranging in ages from Elementary School through High School Students. She has struggled with dissociation most of her life, but writing has allowed her to start the healing process and access once hidden memories. She started blogging as part of her healing process and to help others understand that trauma doesn't mean you can not heal and enjoy intimate activities. The blog started in the beginning of 2019, and has explored topics from first dates; staying safe when going out alone; sharing experiences to empower others; female sexualization; and the importance of consent for all ages.

She plans on fostering teens and preteens that struggle to stay out of the system. She would also like to found a program in a safe open setting to help teens heal using animals and other hands on tools to focus on while having therapists and group settings to work on reminding children of their worth. She is determined to help others not feel so alone in the world. As well as reminding people that they deserve to be loved and respected as they are.

www.ingramcontent.com/pod-product-compliance
Lightning Source LLC
Chambersburg PA
CBHW050727010526
44107CB00009B/759